Exploring Careers for the 21st Century

Second Edition

Entrepreneurship Workbook

Steve Mariotti

Neelam Patel Chowdhary

Betsy Newberry

PEARSON

Cover Art: Courtesy of olesiabilkei/Fotolio, Andres Rodriguez/Fotolia, michaeljung/Fotolia, Monkey Business/Fotolia

Taken from:
Exploring Careers for the 21st Century, Entrepreneurship Workbook
by Steve Mariotti, Betsy Newberry, Neelam Patel
Copyright © 2010 by Pearson Education, Inc.
Published by Prentice Hall
Upper Saddle River, New Jersey 07458

Copyright © 2015 by Pearson Learning Solutions
All rights reserved.

This copyright covers material written expressly for this volume by the editor/s as well as the compilation itself. It does not cover the individual selections herein that first appeared elsewhere. Permission to reprint these has been obtained by Pearson Learning Solutions for this edition only. Further reproduction by any means, electronic or mechanical, including photocopying and recording, or by any information storage or retrieval system, must be arranged with the individual copyright holders noted.

All trademarks, service marks, registered trademarks, and registered service marks are the property of their respective owners and are used herein for identification purposes only.

Pearson Learning Solutions, 501 Boylston Street, Suite 900, Boston, MA 02116
A Pearson Education Company
www.pearsoned.com

000200010271862776
RP

ISBN 10: 1-269-88640-1

ISBN 13: 9-781-269-88640-6

Contents

Introduction iv
Chapter 1: Your Personal Strengths. 1
Chapter 2: The Roles You Play 8
Chapter 3: Why We Work. 16
Chapter 4: Exploring the Career Clusters 24
Chapter 5: Think Like an Entrepreneur 31
Chapter 6: Skills for Success 39
Chapter 7: Academic Planning 46
Chapter 8: Communicating with Others. 54
Chapter 9: Building Relationships. 62
Chapter 10: Basic Math Skills 70
Chapter 11: Technology and Your Career 76
Chapter 12: Career Planning. 84
Chapter 13: Managing a Job Search 94
Chapter 14: Getting Started in Your Career 103
Chapter 15: Being Productive in Your Career 111
Chapter 16: Balancing Work, Family, and Friends 119
Chapter 17: Starting Your Own Business 126
Chapter 18: Planning Your Business 133
Chapter 19: Managing Your Business 150
Chapter 20: Personal Money Management. 157
Chapter 21: Personal Financial Planning 164
Chapter 22: Basic Economics 172
Chapter 23: Basic Business Financial Management 180
Chapter 24: Basic Business Calculations. 187

Introduction

This workbook is designed to reinforce the entrepreneurial concepts that you are learning about in *Exploring Careers for the 21st Century*. You will find many different types of activities per chapter. To use the workbook most effectively:

- Follow the directions. If you are instructed to research a topic on the Internet or in your textbook before completing the activity, be certain to gather all the information you need before you answer.
- Use your text to help you complete the activities.
- Check your answers for accuracy. If you have difficulty with answers, return to the text and read the information again.
- It is very difficult to "play catch-up." Complete the activities when they are assigned.

Note to the teacher: The answer key to the workbook is included as part of the online teacher resources (www.pearsoncustom.com/us/exploringcareers). However, many of the activities in the workbook don't have "correct" answers, so student responses will vary.

Chapter 1: Your Personal Strengths

Name:_____ Date:_____ Period: _____

Matching

Transferable skills can be used in almost any business. They are important to employees, but they are extremely valuable to entrepreneurs in starting up and building a business. Match the transferable skill in the right column to its definition in the left. You may use a dictionary if necessary.

_____ 1. Attempt to come to an agreement through discussion and compromise.

_____ 2. Dealing with a problem successfully.

_____ 3. Skillful handling or use of resources.

_____ 4. Ability to guide, direct, or influence people.

_____ 5. Being accountable to somebody or for something.

_____ 6. Choosing or making determinations in a clear and definite way.

_____ 7. Truthfulness; quality of being fair.

_____ 8. Act of working with others to achieve a common goal.

_____ 9. To feel or show honor, esteem, and consideration for someone else.

_____ 10. Imaginativeness in developing new and original ideas and things.

_____ 11. Freedom from the influence or control of others.

_____ 12. Effective exchange of information between people.

A. Decision making
B. Communication
C. Cooperation
D. Independence
E. Respect
F. Creativity
G. Honesty
H. Management
I. Responsibility
J. Leadership
K. Negotiation
L. Problem solving

Name:_____ Date:_____ Period: _____

Problem Solver

Every entrepreneur understands the importance of employability skills. Employability means having and using your life skills and abilities on the job. Complete the chart below on employability skills.

Employability Skill	Why Is It Important?	How Can It Be Demonstrated?
Positive attitude		
Being cooperative		
Accepting criticism		
Flexibility		
Leadership		

Can you think of any other employability skills? If so, list them here.

_____
_____
_____
_____

Name:_____ Date:_____ Period: _____

Teamwork

Working in small groups, develop a list of Dos (things you should do) and Don'ts (things you should not do) for the workplace. Explain why you listed each item.

Dos	
Things you should do:	Why is this important?
Don'ts	
Things you should not do:	Why shouldn't you do this?

Entrepreneurship Workbook

Name:_____ Date:_____ Period: _____

Critical Thinking

Below is a list of common work values. Refer to page 6 in Chapter 1 if you are unsure what some of these mean. If you were an entrepreneur, which values would be most important to your success? Rank them in order of importance from 1 to 13 with 1 being the most important.

_____ Creativity

_____ Physical activity

_____ Independence

_____ Good salary

_____ Job security

_____ Work environment

_____ Leadership opportunities

_____ Prestige

_____ Challenge

_____ Work safety

_____ Variety

_____ Working with people

_____ Thinking

Explain your rankings.

_____
_____
_____

How will these work values influence the type of business you might choose to start?

_____
_____
_____

Name: _____ Date: _____ Period: _____

Write Now

1. The skills and abilities you gain in activities at school and in the community can help you choose the right business to start. Describe the activities and groups you participate in and what you have learned from them. Explain how these skills and abilities could help you build your own business.

   _____
   _____
   _____
   _____
   _____
   _____
   _____
   _____
   _____
   _____

2. Think about the skills and abilities you would like to develop. What could you do to develop them? Are there activities you could participate in to help you? Are there opportunities available to you for volunteering or community service? If so, describe those and explain your answer.

   _____
   _____
   _____
   _____
   _____
   _____
   _____
   _____
   _____
   _____

Name:_____ Date:_____ Period: _____

Check It

If you were an entrepreneur, which of the following character qualities would you look for in the people you hire? Place a check on the line beside those qualities.

_____ Compassion	_____ Indifference	_____ Laziness	_____ Thoughtfulness
_____ Dishonesty	_____ Intolerance	_____ Meanness	_____ Tolerance
_____ Enthusiasm	_____ Kindness	_____ Stubbornness	_____ Trustworthiness

How did you decide which qualities to select? Explain your answer.

_____
_____
_____
_____

True or False

Circle whether each statement is true or false.

1. True   False   An entrepreneur is a person who organizes and runs his or her own business.
2. True   False   Entrepreneurs almost always work a regular 40-hour work week.
3. True   False   Starting your own business comes with very little risk.
4. True   False   Flexibility is a valuable character quality for an entrepreneur.
5. True   False   Most entrepreneurs start up their own businesses because they want to work for someone else.
6. True   False   Entrepreneurs rarely have to invest any of their own money in starting up their business.
7. True   False   Most entrepreneurs do not receive a regular salary when they first start up their business.
8. True   False   The benefits of being an entrepreneur include the pride and excitement that come with owning your own business.
9. True   False   Identifying strengths and skills can help an entrepreneur choose the right business to start.
10. True   False   Most entrepreneurs are dependent on other people to run their business.

Name:_____ Date:_____ Period: _____

Crossword

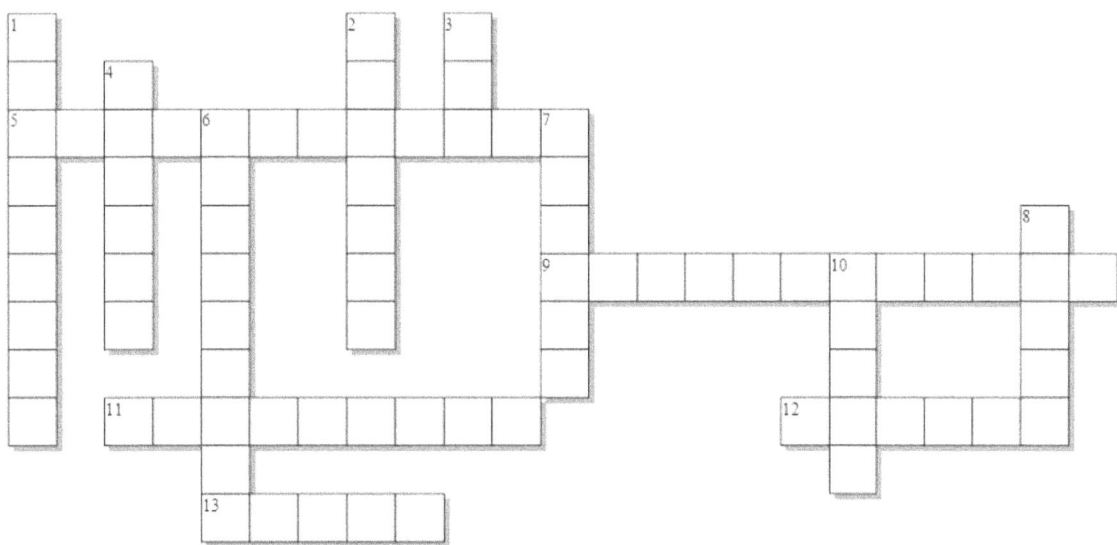

Across:

5. Skills that can be used on almost any job
9. Values based on something important for acquiring something else
11. Your positive qualities and skills
12. The thoughts, ideas, and actions that are important to you
13. An ability or talent

Down:

1. Values based on something important in and of itself
2. Positive character traits
3. An activity that you do in exchange for money or other payment
4. A chosen field of work in which you try to advance over time
6. Guidelines for whether or not something meets expectations
7. A set of beliefs about what is right or wrong
8. The money that you receive in exchange for work performed
10. Values that help you judge behavior based on what you think is right or good

Possible Answers:

career, ethics, instrumental, intrinsic, job, moral, skill, standards, strengths, transferable, values, virtues, wages

Entrepreneurship Workbook   7

Chapter 2: The Roles You Play

Name:_____ Date:_____ Period:_____

Problem Solver

An entrepreneur must play many different roles at work. The table below lists some of these roles. Write about the entrepreneur's responsibilities in each role.

Role	Responsibilities in that Role
Owner	
Manager	
Co-worker	
Employee	

1. Which role do you think would be most challenging for the entrepreneur? Explain your answer.

_____
_____
_____
_____

2. What other roles might an entrepreneur fill at work? List any you can think of below and explain the responsibilities for each.

   _____
   _____
   _____
   _____

3. In the table below, list the roles you fill in the five main areas of your life.

Family	Work	Peers	School	Community

4. Select one of the roles you listed in the table above and explain how your responsibilities in that role can help you succeed as an entrepreneur.

   _____
   _____
   _____
   _____

5. Refer again to the table above. Write about a role that you could add to one of the areas of your life that would help prepare you to start up your own business.

   _____
   _____
   _____
   _____

Name:_____ Date:_____ Period: _____

Critical Thinking

Rules are a necessary part of life. List the rules you are expected to follow in each of the areas listed below. Explain the consequences for breaking each of these rules.

Home and Family Rules	Consequences for Breaking
School Rules	**Consequences for Breaking**
Community Rules	**Consequences for Breaking**

If you owned your own business, what workplace rules would you set for your employees? List them in the table below and explain the reason(s) for making each rule.

Workplace Rules	Reason(s) for Rule

Matching

Match the type of well-being with its definition.

____ 1. Emotional well-being

____ 2. Environmental well-being

____ 3. Intellectual well-being

____ 4. Personal well-being

____ 5. Physical well-being

____ 6. Social well-being

A. Depends on your ability to deal with problems and stress.

B. Depends on your health.

C. Depends on how you get along with other people.

D. Depends on how satisfied and confident you are with yourself.

E. Depends on your ability to think and learn new things.

F. Depends on your comfort and satisfaction with the environment in which you live and work.

Name:_____ Date:_____ Period: _____

Teamwork

Most successful entrepreneurs have well-being in all areas of their lives. Working in groups of two or three, discuss the things an entrepreneur can do to promote his or her well-being in each area. Record your answers below.

1. Emotional well-being

   _____
   _____
   _____

2. Environmental well-being

   _____
   _____
   _____

3. Intellectual well-being

   _____
   _____
   _____

4. Personal well-being

   _____
   _____
   _____

5. Physical well-being

   _____
   _____
   _____

6. Social well-being

   _____
   _____
   _____

Name:_____ Date:_____ Period: _____

Fill in the Blank

Fill in the blank with a word from the box.

Capital	Library	Renewable
Community	Money	Technological
Computer	Natural	Time
Human	Nonrenewable	Water

1. _____ resources are the resources people provide that things cannot.
2. _____ resources include things, such as houses and cars.
3. _____ resources include machines and automation.
4. _____ resources are services that the government provides.
5. _____ resources are things that exist in nature and are available for everyone.
6. _____ resources can be recreated in unlimited quantities.
7. _____ resources are natural resources that are available in limited quantities.
8. _____ is an example of a human resource.
9. _____ is an example of a capital resource.
10. _____ is an example of a natural renewable resource.
11. A _____ is an example of a technological resource.
12. A _____ is an example of a community resource.

Entrepreneurship Workbook

Name:_____ Date:_____ Period: _____

Put It Together

In the table below, list the resources an entrepreneur could use in each of the categories.

Resource Type	Entrepreneur's Resources
Human	
Capital (or nonhuman)	
Technological	
Community	
Natural	

14   Chapter 2

Name:_____ Date:_____ Period: _____

Order of Importance

Below is a list of common resources that an entrepreneur would use. If you were an entrepreneur, which resources would be most important to your success? Rank them in order of importance from 1 to 8 with 1 being the most important.

_____ Money

_____ Health

_____ Knowledge

_____ Time

_____ Talents

_____ Property

_____ Technology

_____ Government/public services

Explain your rankings.

_____
_____
_____
_____
_____
_____

Compare your rankings with those of a classmate. Summarize the similarities and differences.

_____
_____
_____
_____
_____
_____

Chapter 3: Why We Work

Name:_____ Date:_____ Period: _____

Short Answer

Lifestyle factors are the things about your work that affect the way you live your life. Imagine you are an entrepreneur and are set to start up your own business. Describe your ideal or dream situation for each of the following lifestyle factors.

1. **Location.** Where do you imagine yourself living as an adult? Describe the location.

   _____
   _____
   _____
   _____

2. **Work environment.** Would you like to work inside? Outside? Alone? With others? Explain.

   _____
   _____
   _____
   _____

3. **Time.** How many hours per week would you want to work and what time of day would you want to work? Why?

   _____
   _____
   _____
   _____

4. **Salary.** How important is the amount of money you will make? Explain.

   _____
   _____
   _____
   _____

5. **Education.** How much education are you willing to get? Explain.

___

6. Based on your answers to the lifestyle factors, what type of business would meet your dreams? Explain your answer.

___

7. Of all the lifestyle factors listed, in which area would you be the most willing to make concessions, or give up something, to start your dream business? For example, would you be willing to pay yourself a lower salary if it meant you could open your business in the desired location? Explain your answer.

___

8. Of all the lifestyle factors listed, in which area would you be the least willing to make concessions? For example, you might be unwilling to work more than 40 hours a week at your business because you have school and family obligations. Explain your answer.

___

Name:_____ Date:_____ Period: _____

Write Now

Think of something you have that you really wanted and thought you could not live without. Then, answer the questions below.

1. Describe what you wanted.
   _____
   _____
   _____
   _____

2. How long did you have to wait to get it?
   _____
   _____
   _____
   _____

3. Describe how you got the item. Was it a gift? Did you save your money to get it?
   _____
   _____
   _____
   _____

4. Once you got this item, what happened? Was it as good as you had hoped? Did you soon lose interest in it? How often did you use it?
   _____
   _____
   _____
   _____

5. What did you learn from this experience about wants and needs?
   _____
   _____
   _____
   _____

Name:_____ Date:_____ Period: _____

Teamwork

The value of work is measured in many different ways. Some business owners pay themselves a very high salary. Some receive a much smaller salary, but place high value on the benefits their business provides to others. Working in small groups, discuss the value that could be gained from starting each of the following types of business.

Restaurant _____
_____
_____
_____

Graphic design studio _____
_____
_____
_____

Childcare center _____
_____
_____
_____

Career counseling company _____
_____
_____
_____

Home health care company _____
_____
_____
_____

Auto repair and mechanic shop _____
_____
_____
_____

Plumber _____
_____
_____
_____

List two other types of businesses that you would be interested in starting up and explain how you would measure their value.

1. _____

2. _____

What types of businesses do you think are valuable to certain people or to society, but do not make a big profit for their owner? Why do you think this is?

_____

Name:_____ Date:_____ Period: _____

One-on-One

An entrepreneur is someone who starts or owns his or her own business. Interview an entrepreneur and ask the following questions.

1. What business do you own?

   _____
   _____
   _____
   _____

2. Have you owned any other businesses? If so, what were they?

   _____
   _____
   _____
   _____

3. How did you get started with your business?

   _____
   _____
   _____
   _____

4. What were your career goals when you were in school?

   _____
   _____
   _____
   _____

5. What prepared you to start up your own business?

   _____
   _____
   _____
   _____

6. What is your educational background? How has that helped you?

   _____
   _____
   _____
   _____

7. What is the best part of owning your own business?

   _____
   _____
   _____
   _____

8. What are the biggest challenges of owning your own business?

   _____
   _____
   _____
   _____

9. What are your goals for the future of your business?

   _____
   _____
   _____
   _____

10. What advice would you give to someone who wants to start his or her own business?

    _____
    _____
    _____
    _____

Name:_____ Date:_____ Period: _____

True or False

A successful entrepreneur understands the importance of studying trends in the economy, technology, lifestyles, and population. Following are statements on trends. Circle whether each statement is true or false.

1. True False When the economy is strong, there is higher demand for goods and services.

2. True False When the economy is weak, the unemployment rate is low.

3. True False The trend toward storing information and applications on the Internet instead of on local computers is a positive sign for someone wanting to start an information technology business.

4. True False A decreasing number of more traditional work opportunities is a factor that contributes to the increase in entrepreneurship.

5. True False Typically, a rural area will see more new business startups when people leave the area to live in cities.

Fill in the Blank

On the blank, write if the sentence defines an **economic** trend, a **technology** trend, a **lifestyle** trend, or a **demographic** trend.

_____ 1. When the unemployment rate is low, many people are working and earning income. They have money to spend, which increases the demand for goods and services.

_____ 2. An increase in dual-income families results in an increase in the demand for child-care workers.

_____ 3. Improvements in robotics have made it possible to use robots in positions that people once held, such as on automobile assembly lines.

_____ 4. An increasing number of people leaving rural areas to live in cities results in fewer people available to work at rural businesses.

_____ 5. A growing number of employees are now working from a home office, have flexible hours, or even job-share.

Entrepreneurship Workbook   23

Chapter 4: Exploring the Career Clusters

Name:_____ Date:_____ Period: _____

Matching

Match the career cluster with its definition.

____ 1. Decision making about government management and administration.

____ 2. Planning, managing, and providing legal, public safety, and protective services.

____ 3. Managing, marketing, and operating food services, lodging, attractions, and travel-related services.

____ 4. Design, production, exhibition, performance, and publication of things.

____ 5. Planning, managing, and providing scientific research and development.

____ 6. Managing a business's operations.

____ 7. Planning, managing, and performing activities to reach organizational objectives.

____ 8. Production, processing, and development of agricultural resources.

____ 9. Coordinating, managing, and moving goods to their final destinations; also, urban planning.

____ 10. Involved in therapeutic and diagnostic services, health information, and biotechnology research and development.

____ 11. Services for financial and investment banking, insurance products, business/financial management, and so on.

____ 12. Providing services that relate to human needs.

____ 13. Designing, planning, managing, and maintaining the built environment.

____ 14. Planning, managing, and providing education and training.

____ 15. Managing the processes for developing intermediate or final products.

____ 16. Designing, developing, supporting, and managing the systems that connect people and technology.

A. Agriculture, Food & Natural Resources
B. Architecture & Construction
C. Arts, Audio/Video Technology & Communications
D. Business Management & Administration
E. Education & Training
F. Finance
G. Government & Public Administration
H. Health Science
I. Hospitality & Tourism
J. Human Services
K. Information Technology
L. Law, Public Safety, Corrections & Security
M. Manufacturing
N. Marketing
O. Science, Technology, Engineering & Mathematics
P. Transportation, Distribution & Logistics

Name:_____ Date:_____ Period: _____

Multiple Choice

Circle the best response to each question.

1. If you started your own insurance agency, which career cluster would your business fall under?
   A. Education & Training
   B. Government & Public Administration
   C. Finance
   D. Marketing

2. If you worked independently as a carpenter, which career cluster would you be in?
   A. Human Services
   B. Architecture & Construction
   C. Manufacturing
   D. Science, Technology, Engineering & Mathematics

3. Under which career cluster does the occupation of entrepreneur fall?
   A. Business Management & Administration
   B. Hospitality & Tourism
   C. Marketing
   D. Human Services

4. If you started your own fitness center and worked as an athletic trainer in it, which career cluster would you be in?
   A. Hospitality & Tourism
   B. Education & Training
   C. Human Services
   D. Health Science

5. If you opened an ice cream shop, which career cluster would your business fall under?
   A. Business Management & Administration
   B. Marketing
   C. Hospitality & Tourism
   D. Agriculture, Food & Natural Resources

6. If you started a company that designs computer networks for other companies, which career cluster would you be in?
   A. Arts, Audio/Video Technology & Communications
   B. Information Technology
   C. Science, Technology, Engineering & Mathematics
   D. Education & Training

7. If you started a courier service in which you delivered packages for businesses, which career cluster would your business fall under?
   A. Transportation, Distribution & Logistics
   B. Finance
   C. Hospitality & Tourism
   D. Human Services

Entrepreneurship Workbook

Name:_____ Date:_____ Period: _____

Fill in the Blank

Many entrepreneurs follow a specific career pathway before they decide they want to start their own business. Often, it's this experience that helps them form the idea on which they build their business. Below is a list of career pathways. If you followed this pathway, in which career cluster might you start a business? Write the career cluster from the box on the line beside the pathway. You will use each career cluster twice.

Agriculture, Food & Natural Resources

Architecture &Construction

Arts, Audio/Video Technology & Communications

Business Management & Administration

Education & Training

Finance

Government & Public Administration

Health Science

Hospitality & Tourism

Human Services

Information Technology

Law, Public Safety, Corrections & Security

Manufacturing

Marketing

Science, Technology, Engineering & Mathematics

Transportation, Distribution & Logistics

---

1. Performing Arts _____

2. Revenue and Taxation _____

3. Recreation, Amusements and Attractions _____

4. Teaching _____

5. Security and Protective Services _____

6. Professional Sales _____

7. Early Childhood Development and Services _____

8. Food Products and Processing Systems _____

9. Science and Math _____

10. Warehousing and Distribution Center Operations _____

11. Insurance _____

12. Design/Pre-Construction _____

13. Programming and Software Development _____

14. Biotechnology Research and Development _____

15. Maintenance, Installation and Repair _____

16. Human Resources Management _____

---

26   Chapter 4

17. Journalism and Broadcasting _____

18. Foreign Service _____

19. Personal Care Services _____

20. Logistics and Inventory Control _____

21. Professional Support Services _____

22. Plant Systems _____

23. Merchandising _____

24. Web and Digital Communications _____

25. Lodging _____

26. Accounting _____

27. Business Information Management _____

28. Engineering and Technology _____

29. Construction _____

30. Transportation Operations _____

31. Legal Services _____

32. Therapeutic Services _____

Name:_____ Date:_____ Period: _____

Teamwork

The career clusters are designed to help job seekers and individuals identify professions that best suit their interests and needs. Likewise, entrepreneurs can use the career clusters to help them identify the type of business that might best match their skills and interests. Working in small groups, think of a business an entrepreneur could start up within each cluster listed below. Create a name for the business and list what type of business it is. You may review the information provided in the textbook if necessary.

Career Cluster	Name and Type of Business
Agriculture, Food & Natural Resources	
Architecture & Construction	
Arts, Audio/Video Technology & Communications	
Business Management & Administration	
Education & Training	
Finance	

28   Chapter 4

Career Cluster	Name and Type of Business
Government & Public Administration	
Health Science	
Hospitality & Tourism	
Human Services	
Information Technology	
Law, Public Safety, Corrections & Security	
Manufacturing	
Marketing	
Science, Technology, Engineering & Mathematics	
Transportation, Distribution & Logistics	

Name:_____ Date:_____ Period: _____

Critical Thinking

Select two of the career clusters that interest you. Imagine you have just started up a business in the career cluster and you need to hire an employee. What skills, experience, and education will you require? Write your answers in the space below. (You may refer to *careertech.org/career-clusters,* where you can find specific information on knowledge and skills as well as a plan of study for each career cluster.)

Career Cluster 1 _____

Skills, Experience, and Education Required _____

_____

_____

_____

_____

_____

_____

_____

_____

_____

Career Cluster 2 _____

Skills, Experience, and Education Required _____

_____

_____

_____

_____

_____

_____

_____

_____

_____

Chapter 5: Think Like an Entrepreneur

Name:_____ Date:_____ Period: _____

True or False

Circle whether each statement is true or false.

1. True   False   Entrepreneurship is easy, and most new business startups are successful in their first few weeks of operation.
2. True   False   Starting your own business comes with many risks, one of which is the risk of losing money.
3. True   False   Entrepreneurs tend to be creative, hard-working, and willing to take risks.
4. True   False   Because they often work alone, it is not necessary for entrepreneurs to have strong communication skills.
5. True   False   Making money is the only reward for being an entrepreneur.

Fill in the Blank

Fill in the blank with a word from the box.

Business	Intrapreneurship
Employee	Reward
Entrepreneurship	Risk
Income	Social networking

1. _____ is the chance of losing something.
2. Unreliable _____ is when the amount of money you pay yourself changes month to month.
3. A(n) _____ is a benefit an entrepreneur obtains as a result of the job he or she does.
4. A(n) _____ is an organization that provides goods or services, usually to make money.
5. _____ is the process of starting a new business.

Entrepreneurship Workbook

Name:_____ Date:_____ Period: _____

Multiple Choice

Circle the best response to each question.

1. Which of the following choices is not a way to think like an entrepreneur?
    A. See projects through to completion.
    B. Contribute new ideas in class.
    C. Turn in incomplete assignments.
    D. Respect your classmates.

2. Why might an employer like to hire and promote employees who think like an entrepreneur?
    A. They look for chances to learn new skills and accept new responsibilities.
    B. They focus on their own tasks and do not pay attention to what others have to say.
    C. They complain about a problem and expect others to find a solution to it.
    D. They are reluctant to offer feedback and make decisions.

3. Which of the following is not a reward for an entrepreneur?
    A. Build up of a lot of debt.
    B. Pride and personal satisfaction from starting and growing a business.
    C. Ability to make your own rules and set your own schedule.
    D. Opens up opportunities to give back to and improve the community.

4. Which of the following facts about entrepreneurs is accurate?
    A. Very few business owners have any college education when they start their business.
    B. Business owners rarely use money of their own, or from their families, to start or buy the business.
    C. Very few business owners work more than 40 hours per week.
    D. About half of business owners base their business out of their home.

5. Which of the following is not a characteristic of an entrepreneur?
    A. Willing to take risks.
    B. Inflexible and not willing to make changes.
    C. Creative and curious.
    D. Responsible and accountable.

6. Most entrepreneurs need all of the following skills except which one?
    A. Communication skills.
    B. Athletic skills.
    C. Mathematical skills.
    D. Relationship skills.

Name:_____ Date:_____ Period: _____

Teamwork

Imagine you are a member of a school group and you have been invited to visit a school in another country. You must raise the money to make the trip or you cannot go.

Working in small groups, discuss ways you could raise money for your expenses.

1. List the ideas you considered.

   _____
   _____
   _____
   _____
   _____
   _____

2. Which one did you select? Why?

   _____
   _____
   _____
   _____
   _____

3. You will probably need to get permission to proceed. What information will you need to provide to obtain permission? List those items here.

   _____
   _____
   _____
   _____
   _____

4. Within your group, prepare a presentation of your idea that you will use to get permission. Be prepared to present this in class.

___

5. How will you market (advertise) your plan? Describe your plan here. Be prepared to present your plan in class.

___

Name:_____ Date:_____ Period: _____

Short Answer

You can increase your entrepreneurial potential by focusing on the six areas listed below. Write an explanation of the things you can do to build and strengthen your skills in each area.

1. **Business knowledge.** _____
   _____
   _____
   _____

2. **Financial skills.** _____
   _____
   _____
   _____

3. **Career exploration.** _____
   _____
   _____
   _____

4. **Community awareness.** _____
   _____
   _____
   _____

5. **Education.** _____
   _____
   _____
   _____

6. **Relationships.** _____
   _____
   _____
   _____

Name:_____ Date:_____ Period: _____

Critical Thinking

The skills and abilities you gain in activities at school and within the community can help you develop skills you need to start your own business.

List below the activities in which you have participated. Don't forget any volunteer work you have done.

_____   _____
_____   _____
_____   _____
_____   _____

Now refer to the *Short Answer* activity you completed on the previous page. Complete the chart below describing what you have learned or gained from the activities you have participated in.

Business knowledge	
Financial skills	
Career exploration	
Community awareness	
Education	
Relationships	

Name:_____ Date:_____ Period: _____

Thumbs Up! Thumbs Down!

Entrepreneurship has both advantages and disadvantages. For each of the areas of job satisfaction, list the advantages in the Thumbs Up box and the disadvantages in the Thumbs Down box.

1. Overall Job Satisfaction

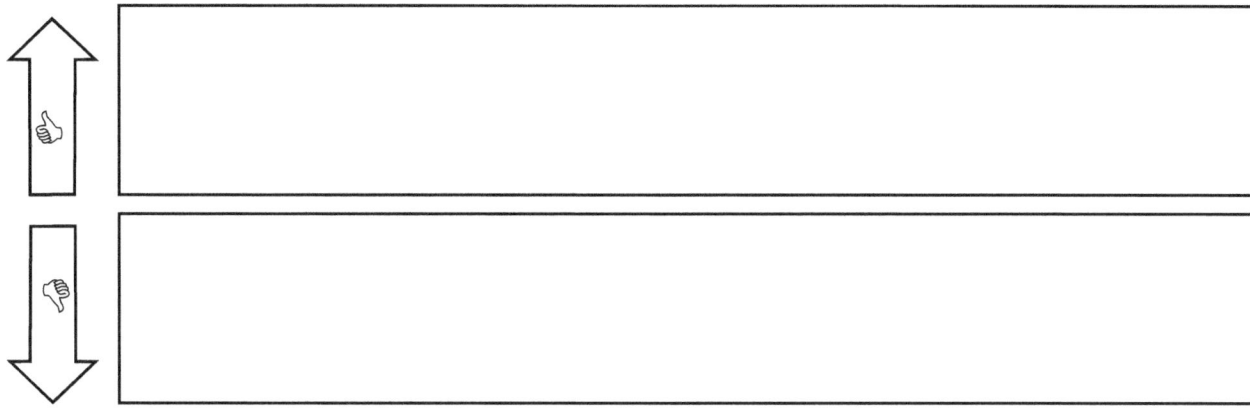

2. Job Security

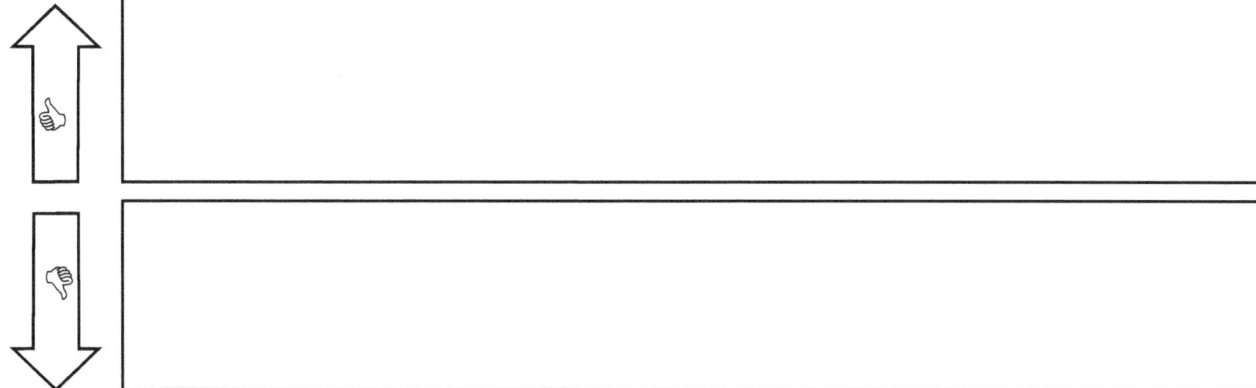

Entrepreneurship Workbook

3. Financial Security and Success

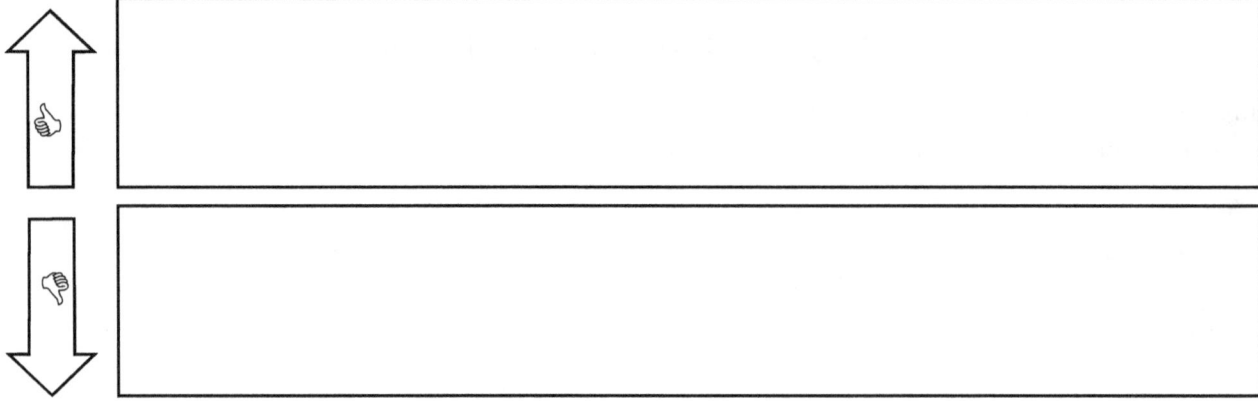

4. Workload and Schedule

Chapter 6: Skills for Success

Name:_____ Date:_____ Period:_____

Put It Together

Successful entrepreneurs understand the importance of strong decision-making skills. Complete the chart below on the six-step decision-making process.

Step	Name the Step	What Does It Involve?	Why Is It Important?
1			
2			
3			
4			
5			
6			

Name:_____ Date:_____ Period:_____

True or False

Circle whether each statement is true or false.

1. True False Making healthy choices will always lead to positive consequences.
2. True False Generally, the person who is blocked from achieving a goal is the one who owns the problem and is responsible for solving it.
3. True False Ignoring your problems shows that you are independent and capable.
4. True False It is always best to solve your problems by yourself because asking for help is a sign of weakness.
5. True False The first step to solving a problem is identifying what the problem is.
6. True False An entrepreneur should set only short-term goals so that he or she can focus on making a profit quickly.
7. True False Breaking long-term goals down into a series of milestones makes it easier to stay on track and achieve them.
8. True False An entrepreneur who hires an employee because he or she thinks the applicant is nice and really needs the money is making a subjective decision.
9. True False Strong critical thinking skills rely largely on a person's emotions and feelings rather than his or her ability to assess something objectively.
10. True False A manager is someone who takes all the credit when something goes right and looks for others to blame when something goes wrong.
11. True False Thinking critically and communicating effectively are important skills for a manager.
12. True False Entrepreneurs who work by themselves do not need strong manager skills.
13. True False Leadership is a skill that people are born with; it is not one that can be developed.
14. True False An entrepreneur who knows how to compromise and communicate exhibits strong leadership skills.
15. True False Effective leaders know their strengths and also their weaknesses.

Name:_____ Date:_____ Period: _____

Self-Evaluation

Complete the following survey. Use this key for your answers:

1—Strongly disagree   2—Disagree   3—Unsure   4—Agree   5—Strongly agree

_____ 1. I take responsibility for my own actions.

_____ 2. Once I make a decision, I do not second-guess it.

_____ 3. I frequently set goals for myself.

_____ 4. When I need to make a decision, I put it off as long as possible.

_____ 5. My friends frequently ask me for advice.

_____ 6. I usually act before I think.

_____ 7. I have good time-management skills.

_____ 8. Before I make a decision, I consider all possible options.

_____ 9. I frequently procrastinate.

_____ 10. I am an honest person.

_____ 11. I try to always do my best.

_____ 12. I frequently let others make decisions for me.

_____ 13. I have people I trust who can give me advice when I need it.

_____ 14. I consider myself an open-minded person.

_____ 15. I am frequently impulsive.

_____ 16. I carefully consider the consequences before I make a decision.

_____ 17. I am usually happy with the decisions I make.

_____ 18. I try to learn from my mistakes.

_____ 19. I am a strong leader.

_____ 20. I am willing to compromise when necessary.

Entrepreneurship Workbook

Name:_____ Date:_____ Period: _____

Sequence

Entrepreneurs must have strong problem-solving skills for their businesses to run smoothly and be successful. Many use the six-step problem-solving process. The steps are listed below but they are not in the correct order. Write the correct number for each step on the blanks.

_____ Make and implement a plan of action.

_____ Select the best solution.

_____ Identify the problem.

_____ Evaluate the solution, process, and outcome.

_____ Consider all possible solutions.

_____ Identify the consequences of each solution.

Fill in the Blank

Fill in the blank with a word from the box.

Consequences	Leader	Objective
Decision	Manager	Problem
Goal	Milestone	Subjective

1. A(n) _____ is a type of manager who unites people to work toward common goals.

2. Being _____ means looking at things fairly and without emotion or prejudice.

3. Being _____ means letting opinions, feelings, and beliefs affect the way you look at things.

4. A(n) _____ is something you are trying to achieve.

5. A(n) _____ is a difficulty or challenge that you must resolve before you can make progress.

6. A(n) _____ is someone who makes decisions, solves problems, and uses resources to achieve specific goals.

7. The results of a decision are called _____.

Name:_____ Date:_____ Period: _____

Teamwork

Read each of the situations below and discuss within your group. Then, answer the questions.

1. You and your friend started up a pet care business in which you take care of pets while the owners are away. You and your friend agreed to equally split the profits, which has been fine until recently when you've been asked to take care of more exotic pets, such as birds, snakes, and lizards. You like being around all kinds of animals but your friend is only comfortable around cats and dogs. You have had to take on the extra business yourself but you and your friend are still splitting the profits evenly.

What is your problem?_____
_____

What are the possible options? _____
_____
_____
_____

What are the short-term consequences of each option? _____
_____
_____
_____
_____

What are the long-term consequences of each option? _____
_____
_____
_____
_____

Which option would you choose? Explain your answer. _____
_____
_____
_____
_____

2. You are a talented artist and recently started a business designing and selling stationary and note cards. You have been successful selling to family and friends through word-of-mouth, but other people have begun buying your products, too. One of your classmates, who is also a good artist, sees your success, starts up the same type of business, and is selling her products for a lower price to many of your customers.

What is your problem? _____

What are the possible options? _____

What are the short-term consequences of each option? _____

What are the long-term consequences of each option? _____

Which option would you choose? Explain your answer. _____

Name:_____ Date:_____ Period: _____

Write Now

Think of people you know who are considered strong leaders. Select one person you think best represents the characteristics of a good leader. Describe that person and the qualities that make him or her a good leader.

_____
_____
_____
_____
_____
_____
_____
_____
_____
_____
_____
_____
_____

How would you rate your leadership skills? In what areas or ways are your leadership skills strong? In what areas are your leadership skills lacking?

_____
_____
_____
_____
_____

How could leadership skills help you as an entrepreneur? Explain your answer.

_____
_____
_____
_____
_____

Entrepreneurship Workbook

Chapter 7: Academic Planning

Name:_____ Date:_____ Period: _____

Multiple Choice

Circle the best response to each question.

1. Which of the following characteristics would discourage a business owner from hiring a job applicant?
   A. Ability to communicate with others.
   B. Good work ethic.
   C. Self-disciplined.
   D. No diploma or degree.

2. A personal academic plan could help you determine the type of business to start because it
   A. includes an assessment of your skills, knowledge, and experience.
   B. lists your personal references.
   C. shows how much money you will make in your career pursuits.
   D. identifies the types of loans you are qualified to get.

3. Why would elective courses help a potential entrepreneur decide on the type of business to start?
   A. They are typically less difficult and easier to get a good grade in.
   B. They provide an opportunity to discover or strengthen your interests.
   C. They focus on standard core subjects.
   D. They teach students how to write a business plan.

4. Which of the following is not a suitable option for continuing your education beyond high school?
   A. Enlisting in the military.
   B. Watching reality TV shows and documentaries.
   C. Enrolling in a technical or vocational program.
   D. Becoming an apprentice.

5. Business owners gain valuable work experience through all of the following except
   A. playing video games.
   B. joining school clubs and organizations.
   C. job shadowing.
   D. participating in mentoring programs.

6. Why are math skills important in any career or business?
   A. They help you create a good resume.
   B. They help you to be organized.
   C. They help you with everyday tasks such as following schedules, taking measurements, and managing money.
   D. They help you communicate effectively.

Name:_____ Date:_____ Period: _____

Self-Evaluation

Complete the following survey to determine your preferred way of learning.

When you…	Do you…		
Spell	Try to see the word? Yes No	Sound out the word? Yes No	Write the word down? Yes No
Are relaxing	Prefer to read a book or watch TV? Yes No	Prefer to listen to or play music? Yes No	Prefer to do some type of physical activity? Yes No
Are in a conversation with others	Listen and observe while others talk? Yes No	Do most of the talking? Yes No	Gesture and move around a lot? Yes No
Get a new piece of equipment or electronic device	Read the instructions that come with it? Yes No	Ask someone to tell you how to operate it? Yes No	Try to figure it out without the instructions? Yes No
Are going to a place you have never been before	Look at a map? Yes No	Ask someone to tell you directions? Yes No	Feel your way and maybe use a compass? Yes No
Teach something	Write down steps for others to follow? Yes No	Explain it verbally? Yes No	Demonstrate it? Yes No
Shop	Browse and envision? Yes No	Ask a store clerk questions? Yes No	Try it on or test it out? Yes No
Try to figure out someone's mood	Study facial expressions? Yes No	Listen to the tone of voice? Yes No	Try to read body movements and body language? Yes No
Are angry	Become silent and brooding? Yes No	Shout or argue about it? Yes No	Clench or pound your fists, or make some other physical outburst? Yes No
Are concentrating	Become distracted by clutter and disorganization? Yes No	Become distracted by sounds or noise? Yes No	Become distracted by movement or activity? Yes No
If you…	Answered "yes" to more questions in this column, you might be a visual learner.	Answered "yes" to more questions in this column, you might be an auditory learner.	Answered "yes" to more questions in this column, you might be a tactile learner.

Entrepreneurship Workbook

Name:_____ Date:_____ Period: _____

Matching

What learning style would characterize a person who starts up a business doing the following? Write **visual**, **auditory**, or **tactile** on the line for each.

_____ 1. Carpenter

_____ 2. Accountant

_____ 3. Translator

_____ 4. Graphic designer

_____ 5. Musician

_____ 6. Architect

_____ 7. Landscaper

_____ 8. Psychologist

_____ 9. Photographer

_____ 10. Writer

_____ 11. Chauffeur

_____ 12. Fashion designer

_____ 13. Actor

_____ 14. Voice instructor

_____ 15. Chef/Restaurant owner

_____ 16. Personal trainer

_____ 17. Mechanic

_____ 18. Lawyer

_____ 19. Composer

_____ 20. Interior decorator

Name:_____ Date:_____ Period: _____

Teamwork

Working in teams, imagine you are the owners of a small business. Select one of the following topics that you must teach to the employees you hire.

- Proper phone etiquette
- How to deposit a check in a checking account
- How to write a memo

Describe below how you would teach this topic using each of the three main learning styles.

Visual: _____

_____

_____

_____

_____

_____

Auditory: _____

_____

_____

_____

_____

_____

Tactile: _____

_____

_____

_____

_____

_____

Name:_____ Date:_____ Period: _____

Crossword

Across:
3. Cost of meals and your dorm room
5. Cost of education, or how much you pay to take classes
9. People who will provide a recommendation for you when you apply for a job or school in the future
10. Someone who works with a professional to learn a skill or trade
11. Careful plans and methods of doing something

Down:
1. Money you are given for college that you do not have to repay
2. Temporary job, usually for students, that might or might not pay a salary
4. Degree that takes four years of study after high school
5. Record of the classes you have taken and the grades you received
6. Helps you set goals for the things you want to accomplish while you are in school
7. Money to help pay for your education
8. Degree that takes two years of study after high school

Possible Answers:

academic plan, apprentice, associate, bachelors, financial aid, grants, internship, references, room and board, strategies, transcript, tuition

50   Chapter 7

Name:_____ Date:_____ Period: _____

Matching

Participating in a career and technical student organization (CTSO) can help you determine the type of business you might like to start up. Below is a list of some national CTSOs. Match the organization to its description. If you're not familiar with any of the organizations, look them up on the Internet.

____ 1. For students in family and consumer sciences programs

____ 2. For students in business, government, and public service programs

____ 3. For students in business and marketing programs

____ 4. For students in health services programs

____ 5. For students in agriculture programs

____ 6. For students in technical, skills, and service programs

A. National Young Farmer Educational Association (NYFEA)

B. Health Occupations Students of America (HOSA)

C. Family, Career, and Community Leaders of America (FCCLA)

D. SkillsUSA

E. Future Business Leaders of America-Phi Beta Lampda (FBLA-PBL)

F. Business Professionals of America (BPA)

Fill in the Blank

Complete the paragraph by filling in each blank with the correct term from the box.

Animals	**Experience**	**Serve**
Babysit	**Guitar**	**Skill**
Entrepreneurial	**Kitchen**	**Teach**

Many teens use _____ skills to create first jobs for themselves. If you have a _____ or ability that other people will pay for, you can gain work _____ by being an entrepreneur. Are you patient, responsible, and good with kids? You can _____. Do you love _____ and exercise? You can walk dogs. Do you know how to play the _____? You can _____ others. Are you comfortable working in a _____? You can wash dishes or _____ at parties.

Entrepreneurship Workbook   51

Name:_____ Date:_____ Period: _____

Critical Thinking

Think about a business you would be interested in starting. Using the Internet or any other resources, answer the following questions.

1. What business would you be most interested in starting as an adult?

   _____

   _____

2. Describe the business and its structure (for example, location, work environment, number of employees, etc.).

   _____

   _____

3. What education is required for you to start this business?

   _____

   _____

4. Where would you like to go to school to get this education?

   _____

   _____

5. What degree would you need?

   _____

   _____

6. What things can you do now to prepare for this type of business venture? For example, could you join a club or volunteer?

   _____

   _____

   _____

   _____

7. What strengths do you have that would help you with this type of business?

   _____
   _____
   _____
   _____
   _____

8. What challenges would you face in starting up and growing this type of business?

   _____
   _____
   _____
   _____
   _____

9. List two short-term goals that would help you prepare to run this type of business.

   _____
   _____
   _____
   _____
   _____

10. List two long-term goals that would help you prepare to run this type of business.

    _____
    _____
    _____
    _____
    _____

Chapter 8: Communicating with Others

Name:_____ Date:_____ Period: _____

Matching

Many of us use expressions or idioms to communicate thoughts and feelings. Listed below are several expressions that you might hear on occasion in a place of business. Match the expression to its meaning.

____ 1. Taking care of business.

____ 2. Time is of the essence.

____ 3. Set the agenda.

____ 4. Run ragged.

____ 5. Back to the drawing board.

____ 6. We're all in the same boat.

____ 7. Bite off more than you can chew.

____ 8. Devil's advocate.

____ 9. Don't put all your eggs in one basket.

____ 10. From rags to riches.

____ 11. Go the extra mile.

____ 12. Haste makes waste.

____ 13. Know the ropes.

____ 14. Method to my madness.

____ 15. Rome was not built in one day.

A. Doing things quickly results in a poor ending.

B. Someone who takes a position for the sake of argument.

C. To decide what other people should discuss and deal with, often in a way that shows you have more authority than them.

D. To take on a task that is way too big.

E. Understand the details.

F. Going above and beyond whatever is required for the task at hand.

G. Everyone here is facing the same challenges.

H. When an attempt has failed and it's time to start over.

I. To keep extremely busy.

J. Do not put all your resources in one possibility.

K. If you want something to be completed properly, then it's going to take time.

L. I'm doing what I'm supposed to be doing.

M. Strange or crazy actions that appear meaningless but in the end are done for a good reason.

N. Timing and meeting all the deadlines are essential and required.

O. To go from being very poor to being very wealthy.

Name:_____ Date:_____ Period: _____

Critical Thinking

Imagine you are the owner of a business. Select one of the expressions listed on the previous page and explain how you could use it to express your thoughts or feelings to employees about the business's operations.

_____
_____
_____
_____
_____

Think of expressions you have heard or use on a regular basis. List them below along with their meaning.

_____
_____
_____
_____

Slang is defined as very casual speech or writing. Using slang is acceptable in casual, social gatherings, but it is not always appropriate in the workplace. List examples of the slang you commonly use. Then, write what you could replace it with if you were in a professional environment.

Slang	Replace

Name:_____ Date:_____ Period: _____

Check It

Entrepreneurs must be good listeners. They must listen to their customers, their employees, their investors, and their suppliers. Without strong listening skills, they run the risk of losing trust and respect, and that can lead to business failure. Place a check beside the items below that indicate good listening skills.

_____ Avoid eye contact.

_____ Repeat the message you hear out loud to make sure you received it correctly.

_____ Doodle and fidget while others are talking.

_____ Make up your mind about the topic or person before the discussion begins.

_____ Let the other person finish speaking before you respond.

_____ Set your preconceived opinions and emotions aside.

_____ Ignore distractions.

_____ Take phone calls and questions from others, even when someone else is talking to you.

_____ Show interest by using eye contact and positive nonverbal messages.

_____ Interrupt often to ask questions or give your opinion.

Being able to identify positive and negative body language is also important to an entrepreneur. You not only gain an understanding of the nonverbal messages you might be sending to others, but you also become aware of the messages or "vibes" others are sending to you. Below is a list of types of body language or nonverbal communications. Place a **P** for positive on the line by positive body language, and an **N** for negative body language.

_____ Active hand gestures that demonstrate you are engaged in the conversation.

_____ Tapping your fingers or foot impatiently.

_____ Folding your arms across your chest.

_____ Maintaining eye contact.

_____ Prolonged or drawn-out staring.

_____ Standing or sitting up straight.

_____ Leaning forward slightly in your seat.

_____ Breaking eye contact and letting your eyes wander around the room.

_____ Holding your chin up with your hand.

Name: _____ Date: _____ Period: _____

Teamwork

In a small business, teamwork and communication are vital to success. Whether you're the owner or an employee, you must be able to cooperate and communicate effectively with others. Working with a classmate, complete the activity below.

Place a folder or other barrier between you and your classmate so you cannot see what the other person is doing. Draw a picture using simple geometric shapes (circles, squares, triangles, etc). When you are done, take turns describing to your partner how to draw the picture you made. You can only give directions. You cannot ask any questions. When you have completed your pictures, remove the barrier and compare pictures.

1. How did your picture compare to the picture your partner drew using your directions? Describe the similarities and the differences.

    _____
    _____
    _____
    _____

2. What made this activity difficult?

    _____
    _____
    _____
    _____

3. What would have made the activity easier?

    _____
    _____
    _____
    _____

4. Rate your partner's directions using the following scale: **1 = impossible to follow; 2 = difficult to follow; 3 = satisfactory; 4 = easy to follow.** Explain your rating.

    _____
    _____
    _____
    _____

5. What could your partner have done to make the directions he or she gave you clearer or easier to follow?

   _____
   _____
   _____
   _____

6. Based on your partner's feedback, rate your communication skills using the following scale: **1 = needs improvement; 2 = satisfactory; 3 = very good.** Explain your rating.

   _____
   _____
   _____
   _____

7. What could you do to improve your communication skills? Explain your answer.

   _____
   _____
   _____
   _____

Name:_____ Date:_____ Period: _____

Short Answer

In the space below, explain what each step in the six-step communication process means.

1. **Be clear.**
   _____
   _____
   _____

2. **Be personal.**
   _____
   _____
   _____

3. **Be positive.**
   _____
   _____
   _____

4. **Get to the point.**
   _____
   _____
   _____

5. **Listen to the response.**
   _____
   _____
   _____

6. **Think before you respond.**
   _____
   _____
   _____

Name:_____ Date:_____ Period: _____

Critical Thinking

You are the owner of a small business with only six employees. Lately, you have noticed that some employees have been coming in late, taking long lunch hours, and leaving earlier than they should. Write a memo to all employees explaining the importance of punctuality and working the required hours.

MEMORANDUM

TO:

FROM:

DATE:

RE:

Name:_____ Date:_____ Period: _____

Chat!

Communication in the workplace has changed over the past few generations. Working in small groups, discuss each of the following changes and explain if you think this is a good change or a bad change.

1. Obtaining information from the Internet instead of from other resources, such as the library and one-on-one conversation with other people.

   _____
   _____
   _____
   _____

2. Talking on a cell phone in public or while with others.

   _____
   _____
   _____
   _____

3. Sending fewer handwritten letters and notes through "snail mail" (regular mail).

   _____
   _____
   _____
   _____

4. Less face-to-face communication and more electronic communication using e-mail, texting, and social networking Web sites.

   _____
   _____
   _____
   _____

Chapter 9: Building Relationships

Name:_____ Date:_____ Period: _____

Networking

Business owners have to develop working relationships with all types of people—from the employee who answers the phones to the technician who services your copier to the bank manager who approves your loan. Imagine you are the owner of a small business and you have developed relationships with the following people. On the blank, write in the name of a person you know who you think would be suitable in that position and explain why you feel that way.

1. Receptionist _____
   _____

2. Public Relations Manager _____
   _____

3. Accountant _____
   _____

4. Office Manager _____
   _____

5. Salesperson _____
   _____

6. Human Resources Manager _____
   _____

7. Computer Systems Consultant _____
   _____

8. Janitor _____
   _____

9. Lawyer _____
   _____

10. Your Second in Command _____
    _____

Name:_____ Date:_____ Period: _____

True or False

Circle whether each statement is true or false.

1. True　False　A relationship is considered functional if only one of the parties gives and receives what he or she needs.
2. True　False　Being the leader of a team means that your opinions are more important than those of the other team members.
3. True　False　Peer pressure is always negative because it interferes with your well-being and goes against your values.
4. True　False　Using your employer's computer to conduct personal business during work hours is an example of unethical behavior.
5. True　False　Technology has generally had a negative impact on worker productivity and made it more difficult for companies to succeed.
6. True　False　Leaving a conflict unresolved is usually the best way to avoid stress, anger, and resentment.
7. True　False　At the root of all conflict is a problem that blocks you from achieving a goal.
8. True　False　Being aggressive and forcing your opinion on others is an example of a negative way to cope with conflict.
9. True　False　Only inflexible and unproductive employees cause problems in the office.
10. True　False　Relationships are a two-way street, which means you must either give more than you receive or take more than you give.
11. True　False　In a successful team relationship, the older, more experienced members of the team do not have to take on as much responsibility as younger, less experienced members.
12. True　False　Being an effective team member means giving your teammates a chance to succeed, even if you don't get along with them.
13. True　False　Every employee at every level of a company has the responsibility to behave ethically.
14. True　False　Conflicts can occur in both functional and dysfunctional relationships.
15. True　False　Finding common bonds with co-workers will almost certainly result in conflicts.

Name:_____ Date:_____ Period: _____

Critical Thinking

Imagine you are an entrepreneur who has just learned that a group of investors is willing to fund the startup of your business. They were impressed with the business plan you developed. Now, they want to know more about you. After all, they hope this will be the beginning of a long and prosperous relationship! Below is the beginning of a letter to the group of investors. Complete the letter by discussing the skills and qualities you have to run the business. You will want to touch upon your ability to make decisions, solve problems, and motivate others.

Dear Investor:

Thank you for your investment in my company. As you saw in my business plan, the startup costs are minimal and I anticipate that the company will generate a profit by month six of operation. This is an exciting venture and I am looking forward to a long and successful relationship with you. I'd like to take the opportunity now to tell you more about myself.

_____

_____

_____

_____

_____

_____

_____

_____

_____

_____

_____

_____

_____

_____

Name:_____ Date:_____ Period: _____

Teamwork

Whether you are the owner of a business or an employee at any level, you are part of a team. A successful team relationship depends on all team members working together. In this activity, work in small teams to find the following items. Take a few minutes before you begin to strategize.

1. Safety pin
2. Gum wrapper
3. Cup
4. School or college logo
5. Photograph of a famous person
6. Unused pencil
7. Shoe that has red on it
8. Stamp
9. Plastic spoon, knife, or fork
10. Piece of yarn or ribbon

Now answer the following questions. Explain your answers.

1. What was your team's goal? _____
   _____

2. How did you delegate duties? _____
   _____
   _____
   _____

3. How did your group go about finding the items? What was your strategy? _____
   _____
   _____
   _____
   _____

4. Which items did you find? _____
   _____
   _____
   _____
   _____

5. Did everyone in your group participate? Why or why not? _____
_____
_____
_____
_____

6. How successful was your group? _____
_____
_____
_____
_____

7. What could you have done differently to be more successful? _____
_____
_____
_____
_____

8. What did you learn from this activity? _____
_____
_____
_____
_____

Name:_____ Date:_____ Period: _____

Teamwork

Imagine you are starting a new business. Your group is the management team of this business, and you have been given the task of developing a code of ethics for the company. Write the code of ethics below. When you are done, work on your own to answer the questions that follow.

Code of Ethics

_____
_____
_____
_____
_____
_____
_____
_____
_____
_____
_____
_____
_____
_____
_____

Entrepreneurship Workbook

1. Why is it important for a business to have a code of ethics?

2. Would the type of business you own matter when setting your code of ethics? Explain.

3. What are the similarities and differences between the business's code of ethics and the code of ethics at your school?

4. What are the similarities and differences between the business's code of ethics and your own personal set of ethics?

Name:_____ Date:_____ Period: _____

Check It

Place a check beside the items below that indicate a healthy relationship.

____ 1. You make time to help your co-worker with a project, and she makes time to help you.

____ 2. Your employer asks you to work late and pays you for the additional hours.

____ 3. You expect others to provide constant reassurance about your appearance, personality, and abilities.

____ 4. You require others to share your values and standards.

____ 5. You expect to exchange resources equally, and to give as much as you receive.

____ 6. You are willing to discuss your differences.

____ 7. You do what you think is best, even if the rest of the team has a different plan.

____ 8. You do something that interferes with your well-being because another person pressured you into doing it.

____ 9. You give the other person a chance to express his or her opinion on a source of conflict.

____ 10. You avoid employees from different cultures and backgrounds.

Fill in the Blank

Complete the paragraph by filling in each blank with a term from the box.

Communicate	**Entrepreneurs**	**Large**
Conflict	**Investors**	**Relationships**
Employees	**Isolate**	**Small**

_____ are more involved in the day-to-day operations of their business than owners and managers are at a(n) _____ company. Entrepreneurs interact with their _____ on a regular basis, and must be able to build _____ with everyone. Often, the success of the start-up business depends on the entrepreneur's ability to _____, resolve _____, and work together with his or her employees.

Entrepreneurship Workbook   69

Chapter 10: Basic Math Skills

Name:_____ Date:_____ Period: _____

Preparing Invoices

You are the owner of a music shop that sells various instruments and provides music lessons. Complete the following two invoices.

1. Bill this customer for 8 one-hour violin lessons at $30 each. She also bought a set of violin strings for $40 and a new chin rest for $19.

My Music Shop				
Quantity	Description	Unit Price		Total
		Subtotal		
		Sales Tax (7%)		
		TOTAL		

2. Bill this customer for four piano lessons at $25 each. He also bought a beginner piano book for $8.50 and a piano tuning kit for $74.

My Music Shop				
Quantity	Description	Unit Price		Total
		Subtotal		
		Sales Tax (7%)		
		TOTAL		

Name:_____ Date:_____ Period: _____

Let's Go Shopping

You just signed a lease for a building in which you are going to open your own restaurant. You go shopping at several restaurant supply stores and find some really good sales. Calculate the answers to the following problems. Show your work.

1. You find a microwave that's the perfect size for the space you have. The regular price is $279. Today, it is 20 percent off. What is the sale price?

2. You find a sale on frying pans where you buy one for $19.50 and get a second at half price. What will be your total (before tax) if you buy eight pans?

3. You buy eight tables for customer seating. The store has a special on chairs where you can buy one for $40 or you can buy a set of four for $140. You need four chairs for six of the tables and five chairs for two of the tables. How many chairs total do you need? What would be the best deal?

4. You have a coupon worth $20 off your total bill at one store. You buy 30 tablecloths at $3.75 each; 20 centerpieces at $6.29 each; 15 water pitchers at $4.99 each; and 25 sets of salt and pepper shakers at $2.89 each. What is your total bill after the $20 coupon has been deducted?

5. You spend $125.25 on cleaning supplies. If your state sales tax is 6 percent, how much will your bill total?

Entrepreneurship Workbook

Name:_____ Date:_____ Period: _____

Ratios and Proportion

You run a bakery and often get special orders that require you to modify your recipes. Calculate the answers to the following problems.

1. A customer has ordered 90 toffee bars for a corporate sales meeting. Your recipe below yields 30 bars. By how much will you have to increase the ingredients? Fill in the table with the new quantities.

Original Recipe	Adjustment	New Quantity
½ cup butter		
½ cup sugar		
¼ teaspoon salt		
1 cup flour		
1 14-ounce can sweetened condensed milk		
2 teaspoons vanilla		
1 ounce unsweetened chocolate		
1½ cups powdered sugar		

2. The local Chamber of Commerce is having a scholarship lunch and has ordered 4 dozen lemon tea cookies. Your recipe below yields 96 cookies. By how much will you have to decrease the ingredients? Fill in the table with the new quantities.

Original Recipe	Adjustment	New Quantity
2 teaspoons shredded lemon peel		
4 teaspoons lemon juice		
⅔ cup milk		
1 cup butter		
3½ cups flour		
2 cups sugar		
2 eggs		
2 teaspoons baking powder		

Name:_____ Date:_____ Period: _____

Fill in the Blank

Complete each sentence with a term from the box.

Difference	Product	Statistics
Fraction	Proportion	Sum
Geometry	Quotient	
Percentage	Ratio	

1. When you add numbers, the result is called the _____.
2. When you subtract numbers, the result is called the _____.
3. When you multiply numbers, the result is called the _____.
4. When you divide numbers, the result is called the _____.
5. _____ is the math that deals with the size, position, and shape of objects.
6. A(n) _____ is a comparison of two whole numbers.
7. You can calculate a(n) _____ by dividing the amount you have by the total amount, and then multiplying the quotient by 100.
8. A(n) _____ compares two numbers.
9. A(n) _____ is when you have two ratios that equal each other.
10. _____ is a type of math used to collect, organize, and analyze data.

Complete the following paragraph by filling in each blank with a term from the box.

Current ratio	Quick ratio
Operating ratio	Return on sales ratio

Entrepreneurs use different ratios to analyze financial data. For example, the _____ shows the percentage of each dollar of sales needed to cover expenses. The _____ is calculated by dividing net profit by sales. It is a measure of a company's profitability. The _____ compares cash to debt. This ratio is often used by creditors to measure the financial strength or weakness of a company. The _____ shows current assets divided by current liabilities. This ratio measures a company's ability to meet short-term debt obligations.

Entrepreneurship Workbook

Name:_____ Date:_____ Period: _____

Completing Timesheets

You own a small manufacturing company that makes parts for printing presses. Complete the following timesheets.

David Fernandez	Regular Hours	Overtime	Sick	Vacation	Holiday	Total
Monday	0	0	0	0	4	
Tuesday	8	0	0	0	0	
Wednesday	8	2	0	0	0	
Thursday	4	0	4	0	0	
Friday	0	0	0	8	0	
Saturday	0	6	0	0	0	
Sunday	0	3	0	0	0	
Total hours						
Rate per/hr	$18.00	$27.00	$18.00	$18.00	$36.00	
Total pay						

Leah Jackson	Regular Hours	Overtime	Sick	Vacation	Holiday	Total
Monday	0	0	0	0	8	
Tuesday	8	0	0	0	0	
Wednesday	8	0	0	0	0	
Thursday	8	3	0	0	0	
Friday	8	0	0	0	0	
Saturday	0	8	0	0	0	
Sunday	0	0	0	0	0	
Total hours						
Rate per/hr	$22.00	$33.00	$22.00	$22.00	$44.00	
Total pay						

Name:_____ Date:_____ Period: _____

Data Analysis

You own a florist shop and want to analyze your yearly expenses. Your expenses for the current year and previous year are shown in the table below. Determine the total expenses for the current year. Then, determine the percentage of the whole that each expense category represents. Round the percentage to the nearest whole number.

Expense	Previous Year Total	Percent of Total	Current Year Total	Percent of Total
Rent	$1,200.00	15%	$1,200.00	
Utilities	$405.00	5%	$475.00	
Salaries	$3,800.00	47%	$4,100.00	
Flowers from wholesaler	$1,980.00	25%	$2,250.00	
Supplies	$690.00	9%	$750.00	
Total	$8,075.00			

1. In the space below, draw a pie chart that illustrates the percent of total data for the current year.

2. In the space below, draw a column chart that compares the expense categories from the previous year to those for the current year.

Entrepreneurship Workbook

Chapter 11: Technology and Your Career

Name:_____ Date:_____ Period: _____

Matching

Technology has a huge impact on the way you do business, regardless of the type of company you own. Even if you run a farm and work out in the field all day, you must have an understanding of how technology in other areas can help your business succeed. Match each of the technologies listed below to its definition or application.

_____ 1. Enables people to meet "face-to-face" without having to travel any distance at all.

_____ 2. Allows more than one person to work on a document or file at one time.

_____ 3. Enables employees equipped with a phone, computer, and Internet service to work from home.

_____ 4. Allows you to connect to the Internet without having to be connected to any wires or cords.

_____ 5. Software that is programmed to complete tasks that are repetitive, time-consuming, and boring.

_____ 6. Type of computing in which files that are traditionally stored on a computer are stored online and accessed through the Internet.

_____ 7. Computer programs written especially for problem solving.

_____ 8. Computerized system that automatically orders inventory at the exact right time and only for the exact right amount.

_____ 9. Buying and selling of goods and services over the Internet.

_____ 10. Technology that treats fruit and other food products to kill bacteria and insects.

_____ 11. Helps people track their appointments and business contacts.

_____ 12. Sending small written messages from one cell phone to another.

A. Algorithm
B. Automation software
C. Cloud computing
D. Collaborative software
E. E-commerce
F. Irradiation
G. Just-in-time system
H. Personal digital assistant
I. Telecommuting
J. Texting
K. Videoconferencing
L. Wi-Fi

Name:_____ Date:_____ Period:_____

Multiple Choice

Circle the best response to each question.

1. Which of the following technologies would you use if you wanted to cut down on the costs of traveling to client offices but still meet face-to-face with them?

    A. Manufacturing

    B. Telecommuting

    C. E-commerce

    D. Videoconferencing

2. If you wanted a team of employees to have the ability to work on an important client document at the same time, which technology would you use?

    A. Collaborative software

    B. Algorithms

    C. E-commerce

    D. Videoconferencing

3. Many business owners avoid the costs of renting a space for their business by allowing employees to work from home. What is this called?

    A. Telecommuting

    B. Collaborative commuting

    C. E-commerce

    D. Just-in-time job sharing

4. Which of the following technologies would you use to ensure that all your company's computers are automatically backed up on a regular schedule?

    A. Collaborative software

    B. Automation software

    C. Data entry

    D. Wi-Fi

5. Which of the following technologies allows an entrepreneur to connect to the Internet without the use of cords or wires?

    A. Videoconferencing

    B. Telecommuting

    C. Wi-Fi

    D. Irradiation

6. What can you use to conduct more powerful Internet searches?

    A. Collaborative software

    B. Boolean operators

    C. Keyboarding skills

    D. Social networking sites

7. If you were on a job site and needed to be able to make phone calls, send text messages, connect to the Internet, and access files on a computer, which technology would be most helpful?

    A. Smartphone

    B. Automation software

    C. E-mail

    D. Cloud computer

Entrepreneurship Workbook

Name:_____ Date:_____ Period: _____

One on One

Interview someone who is at least 40 years old, asking him or her the following questions. Record the answers below.

1. What technologies are available today that were not available when you were a teenager?

   _____
   _____
   _____
   _____

2. Of the new technologies now available, which do you use on a regular basis at your workplace?

   _____
   _____
   _____
   _____

3. How difficult was it for you to learn how to use the new technology? How did you learn?

   _____
   _____
   _____
   _____

4. Do you think technology has made your life easier? Has technology made your job easier? Explain.

   _____
   _____
   _____
   _____

Name:_____ Date:_____ Period: _____

Yes or No?

The Internet can be a very useful and productive tool for an entrepreneur, but it can also slow you down if you are unfocused or let it distract you. Read each of the following. Circle **Yes** if it is a wise use of technology and **No** if it is not.

1. Yes   No   You browse for current information on your competitors.
2. Yes   No   You play Internet games and visit gossip blogs instead of industry and company Web sites.
3. Yes   No   You instant message with your friends while meeting with a client.
4. Yes   No   You research business opportunities in markets around the world.
5. Yes   No   You send photos of your birthday party the night before to all your employees.
6. Yes   No   You use social networking sites to advertise your company and share ideas with other entrepreneurs.
7. Yes   No   You post personal information about your customers on your company's Web site.
8. Yes   No   You forward spam to your employees and suppliers.
9. Yes   No   You start a blog in which you discuss your company's products and services.
10. Yes   No   You download annual reports and other information on public companies within your industry.

Fill in the Blank

Complete the following paragraph by filling in each blank with a term from the box.

Assembly lines	**E-commerce**	**Inventory**	**Robots**
Auctions	**Encryption**	**Online**	**Scanners**

Many entrepreneurs rely heavily on _____ for their business to succeed, but many technological breakthroughs had to happen before widespread use of this technology became possible. Mathematicians invented _____ software to keep credit card numbers safe. Systems engineers invented computerized _____ systems to keep track of products and orders. Even the handheld _____ that your local package delivery employees use are important because they allow suppliers to instantly see that you have received your products. Now, many companies can avoid the high costs of having a physical storefront; instead they sell their products and services _____.

Entrepreneurship Workbook   79

Name:_____ Date:_____ Period: _____

Teamwork

Technology is a part of our everyday lives. Working in small groups, discuss how technology affects each of the following parts of your lives and record your answers below.

1. How you communicate

   _____
   _____
   _____

2. How you shop

   _____
   _____
   _____

3. How you are entertained

   _____
   _____
   _____

4. How you learn

   _____
   _____
   _____

5. How you exercise

   _____
   _____
   _____

6. How you bank and pay bills

   _____
   _____
   _____

7. How you research

   _____
   _____
   _____

8. How you travel

   _____
   _____
   _____

9. How you search for a job

   _____
   _____
   _____

10. Can you think of other ways you use technology in your everyday life? List them here.

    _____
    _____
    _____

Name:_____ Date:_____ Period: _____

Matching

Entrepreneurs often have to wear many hats. For that reason, they benefit greatly from being familiar with different types of computer applications. Match the computer applications below with their definitions.

____ 1. Allows the user to write letters, memos, reports, and other documents and quickly edit and format them.

____ 2. Allows the user to create and produce slide shows that are helpful for illustrating certain types of information.

____ 3. Allows the user to organize, calculate, and analyze volumes of numbers and data.

____ 4. Allows the user to view and download information stored on the Internet.

____ 5. Allows the user to store, manage, and manipulate records on all facets of the business.

____ 6. Allows the user to create and design content to be viewed online.

____ 7. Allows the user to create sophisticated art and graphics as well as enhance and manipulate photographs.

____ 8. Allows the user to place type and graphics on pages for publications.

A. Database management
B. Graphic design
C. Page layout
D. Presentation
E. Spreadsheet
F. Web browser
G. Web design
H. Word processing

Name: _____ Date: _____ Period: _____

Short Answer

Think of a small business in your community with which you are familiar. Answer the questions below.

1. What is the name of the business? _____
   _____

2. What does the business do? _____
   _____
   _____

3. How are you familiar with the business? _____
   _____
   _____
   _____

4. List and explain three ways the business uses technology in its operations. _____
   _____
   _____
   _____
   _____
   _____
   _____
   _____

5. If you were the owner of the business, what technology would you introduce (or expand the use of) to grow the business? Explain your answer. _____
   _____
   _____
   _____
   _____
   _____

Entrepreneurship Workbook

Chapter 12: Career Planning

Name:_____ Date:_____ Period: _____

Self-Evaluation

The interests, talents, and abilities you develop now might be the only inspiration you need to start your own business in the future! Complete the following survey using the key below to rate each item.

1—Definitely, that's me!   2—Describes me somewhat   3—Unsure   4—No way, not me!

_____ 1. I am artistic and creative.

_____ 2. I am good at seeing how things fit together or come apart.

_____ 3. It is important to me to be able to use my creativity in my work.

_____ 4. I am good at managing and encouraging others.

_____ 5. I am a good organizer.

_____ 6. I enjoy managing money.

_____ 7. I enjoy coming up with new ideas.

_____ 8. I like to travel.

_____ 9. I enjoy working with large groups of people.

_____ 10. I would like to work from home.

_____ 11. I am a good writer.

_____ 12. I love math and science.

_____ 13. I would enjoy a job that requires me to give presentations.

_____ 14. I am a very competitive person.

_____ 15. I am very athletic.

_____ 16. I would like a job that allows me to work outside.

_____ 17. I am willing to go to school for a long time to be qualified to do my job.

_____ 18. I am good at selling things.

_____ 19. I enjoy helping others.

_____ 20. I am a very persuasive person.

____ 21. I enjoy doing research.

____ 22. I am a very patient person.

____ 23. I am good with children.

____ 24. I get along well with most everyone I meet.

____ 25. I am good with animals.

____ 26. I am good at solving problems.

____ 27. I prefer to work alone.

____ 28. I would like a job that allows me to do scientific experiments.

____ 29. I would like a job that requires me to dress professionally.

____ 30. I would like a job that requires me to wear a uniform.

____ 31. I would like to work in the medical field.

____ 32. I would like to work in education.

____ 33. I would like a job that gives me lots of prestige.

____ 34. I would like to work in a service profession.

____ 35. It is more important for me to enjoy my job than to make lots of money.

____ 36. I would like to work at night.

____ 37. I would like a job that has flexible hours.

____ 38. I would like a job that makes me famous.

Review the completed survey. Circle the items that you rated with a "1." Based on the items you circled, list the types of businesses you have the interests, talents, and abilities to start in the space below.

_____
_____
_____
_____
_____
_____
_____

Entrepreneurship Workbook

Name:_____ Date:_____ Period: _____

Critical Thinking

Networking is a valuable tool whether you are looking for a job or preparing to start up your own business. Imagine you have a great idea for a new business. Who in your network of contacts can help you turn your idea into a reality?

1. List all the people you know who can help you develop your idea. List only those people you know *personally*; it's okay if you list only your parents or another relative.

   _____
   _____
   _____

2. List all the people your parents know who could help. This list might include their banker, financial planner, or a business associate.

   _____
   _____
   _____

3. List all the people your friends know who could help. This list might include relatives, teachers, or the people your friends' parents work with.

   _____
   _____
   _____

4. List all the people your neighbors know who could help. This list might include relatives, co-workers, and friends.

   _____
   _____
   _____

Name:_____ Date:_____ Period: _____

Career Plan

You learned in the text that a career plan can help you find a career or career cluster that suits your skills and interests. A career plan is also a useful tool for entrepreneurs. If your career goal is to own your own business, then you can use your career plan to map out a strategy for achieving that goal. Think of a business you would like to own. Complete the career plan on the following pages.

Career Goal

Write a statement that describes your long-term ultimate career goal. (For example: *I will own a bookstore in Boston by the time I am 25 years old.*) _____

_____

_____

_____

Requirements to Meet Career Goal

To achieve my career goal, I need to pursue the following education beyond high school:

_____

_____

_____

To achieve my career goal, I need to have the following skills:

❏ Organizing and allocating resources

❏ Working with others

❏ Acquiring, processing, and evaluating information

❏ Managing social, organizational, and technological systems

❏ Using and applying technology

❏ Other (list below)

_____

_____

_____

_____

Entrepreneurship Workbook

Knowledge and Experience

School classes that will help me achieve my career goal:

Class	Skills Acquired	Date or Grade Level When Class Taken

School activities that will help me achieve my career goal:

Activity	Skills Acquired	Dates or Grade Level(s) for Participation in Activity

Out-of-school activities that will help me achieve my career goal:

Activity	Skills Acquired	Dates for Participation in Activity

Work experiences that will help me achieve my career goal:

Job or Work Experience	Skills Acquired	Date Worked

Awards and accomplishments related to my career plan:

Award or Accomplishment	Date Received

Portfolio items related to my career plan:

Item	Description

Personal

I have the following personal skills, talents, and work habits that will help me achieve my career goal:

_____   _____
_____   _____
_____   _____
_____   _____

I need to strengthen the following skills and work habits to achieve my career goal:

Skill or Habit	Steps I Will Take to Strengthen It

Plan to Reach My Career Goal

To reach my ultimate career goal, I will meet the following short-term goals:

1. _____
2. _____
3. _____
4. _____
5. _____

Name:_____ Date:_____ Period: _____

Short Answer

Using your completed career plan, create your ideal job. Answer the questions below.

1. Describe your business (its location and physical structure).
   _____
   _____
   _____

2. As owner, what would your responsibilities be?
   _____
   _____
   _____

3. What type of schedule would you work, or how many hours a week?
   _____
   _____
   _____

4. Would you work alone, with a few people, or with a large group?
   _____
   _____
   _____

5. How much would you pay yourself, or would you like to pay yourself?
   _____
   _____
   _____

6. What is the biggest benefit of owning this business?
   _____
   _____
   _____

7. What is the biggest challenge of owning this business?

8. Your business is a huge success and you need to hire employees in all areas. Write a general help wanted ad that focuses on the nature of your business and why it would be a great place to work.

Chapter 13: Managing a Job Search

Name:_____ Date:_____ Period: _____

Check It

Imagine you are the owner of a small business and need to hire a new employee. You have several candidates you want to interview. Your questions should focus on the candidates' education, past experience, career goals, and questions specific to the job for which they are applying. In general, you should not ask questions relating to a candidate's national origin, citizenship, age, marital status, disabilities, arrest and conviction record, military discharge status, race, gender, or pregnancy status. Any question that asks a candidate to reveal information about these topics could be a violation of state or federal laws. Read the questions below. Place a check on the line by the questions that would be appropriate for you to ask a job applicant.

_____ 1. What do you know about our company, and why do you want to work here?

_____ 2. What are your religious beliefs?

_____ 3. Are you single, married, or divorced?

_____ 4. Why did you leave your last job, and what have you been doing since?

_____ 5. Have you ever been arrested or convicted of a crime?

_____ 6. What would you have changed about your last job and why?

_____ 7. What were your most significant contributions and accomplishments in your previous job?

_____ 8. What is your nationality?

_____ 9. How would you handle a situation that you felt was unethical?

_____ 10. Tell me about an important business decision you made and how you arrived at it.

_____ 11. What do you think are the characteristics of a strong manager?

_____ 12. How do you think your previous co-workers would describe you?

_____ 13. Do you have any disabilities?

_____ 14. What is the most satisfying achievement of your career?

_____ 15. What political party do you belong to?

_____ 16. Do you have children? If not, do you want to have children?

Name:_____ Date:_____ Period: _____

Critique

As a business owner, you can use a cover letter and resume as good measures of a job applicant's ability to express thoughts in writing. They can also demonstrate an applicant's attention to detail and willingness to invest time and energy to make a good first impression. Imagine you are the owner of a small business and received the following letter and resume from job applicants. Circle the errors and other things that you feel make a negative impression.

Oct. 3, 2015

Ms. Helen White
MNO Company
4671 Highland Ave.
Palatine, IL 60067

Hi Helen!

I'm writting to see if you have any jobs open. I thought I'd send my resume in case you did. I'd like to work in humen resourses.

For the past two years, I been working as an acount assistant at Employ Action. An employment agency. In that time, I learn a great deal about employment options and oportunities. I am a hard worker who is looking for new challanges. I also really love football.

I would welcome the opportunity to speak with you personelly about availabel positions. You can contact me by phone or e-mail using the information below.

I would appreciate it!

Love,

Claire Duggan ☺

Claire Duggan
2323 McCloud St.
Palatine, IL 60067
555-555-5555
Claireduggan@mail.net

Entrepreneurship Workbook

Claire Duggan
2556 Granger Ave.
Palatine, IL 60067
(555) 555-5555
claireduggan@mail.net

Objective   *To work as a partime sales asociate in a fashion clothing store.*

Education   Currently enrolled in Wickham High School; <u>hope</u> to graduate in June 2013.

<u>**Work Experience**</u>

9/14-present   Fashun consultint, HH Shelter for Women and Children, Palantine, IL

- Select and coordinate outfits for woman preparing for job interviews.

5/13   Fashion show organizer, Wickham High School, Palantine, IL

- Proposed, plan, and managed fashion show of student designs to raize funds for the HH Shelter for Women and Children.

<u>*Skills*</u>

- Sewing
- Clothing coordination and fit
- <u>*Basic math skills*</u>
- Fluent in Spanish

Extracurricular Activities

   None

What is your general assessment of the cover letter? _____
_____
_____
_____
_____
_____

Would you hire this person? Why or why not? _____
_____
_____
_____
_____
_____
_____

What is your general assessment of the resume? _____
_____
_____
_____
_____
_____

Would you hire this person? Why or why not? _____
_____
_____
_____
_____
_____

Name:_____ Date:_____ Period: _____

Apply It!

Business cards are an important way to expand your network of contacts. For business owners, they are a convenient way to get company information into your customers', or potential customers', hands. Think of a business you would like to start. Then design your company's business card in the space below.

┌─────────────────────────────────┐
│   │
│   │
│   │
│   │
│   │
│   │
└─────────────────────────────────┘

Explain why you designed your business card the way you did.

_____
_____
_____
_____
_____

Name:_____ Date:_____ Period: _____

Short Answer

Like job applicants, entrepreneurs find that job references can be helpful resources when they're trying to secure a loan or convince investors to fund their business. Fill in the following information.

1. Briefly describe the purpose of a reference.
   _____
   _____

2. Give examples of people who would be a good reference.
   _____
   _____

3. Give examples of people you should not ask to be a reference.
   _____
   _____

4. In the table below, list three people you can use as a reference. Include the following information for each reference.

Name	Occupation	Mailing Address	E-mail Address	Phone

Entrepreneurship Workbook

Name:_____ Date:_____ Period: _____

Write Now

One sign of a well-written cover letter and resume is the use of action words to describe skills and experience. Rewrite the following using action words.

1. Can sew _____

2. Have babysat _____

3. Know first-aid _____

4. Helped teacher _____

5. On yearbook staff _____

6. Team manager _____

7. Can cook _____

8. Good in math _____

9. Now think of two skills or areas of experience that you have and describe those using action words.

   _____
   _____
   _____
   _____

Name:_____ Date:_____ Period: _____

Yes or No

A job interview can be stressful for both the person being interviewed and the person asking the questions. Read the statements below. Circle **Yes** if it is something you should do in an interview. Circle **No** if it is not.

1. Yes   No   Dress neatly and professionally and make sure your clothes are clean and appropriate for the workplace.
2. Yes   No   Use slang and be casual about your speech to make the other person feel comfortable.
3. Yes   No   Shoot for being a minute or two late to allow the other person a little extra time to get there.
4. Yes   No   Shake hands with the other person when you first meet and again when the interview is over.
5. Yes   No   Avoid making eye contact when you speak because the other person might think you are staring.
6. Yes   No   If the other person asks you a difficult question, try to hide the fact that you do not know the answer.
7. Yes   No   Ask personal questions regarding the other person's marital status, family, income, and political views.
8. Yes   No   Listen carefully, using positive body language, such as smiling and leaning forward slightly when the other person is talking.
9. Yes   No   Avoid chewing gum, cell phone calls, and texting during the interview.
10. Yes   No   In answering a question, provide as much information on anything you can think of related to the question. Being brief can indicate you do not care or do not know the answer to the question.
11. Yes   No   Avoid fidgeting and playing with your hair or your clothing and jewelry.
12. Yes   No   Speak in a soft, meek voice so you do not appear bold and aggressive.
13. Yes   No   Wear clothing with bright, contrasting colors to get attention and keep the other person focused on you.
14. Yes   No   Avoid questions about the other person's ethnicity, nationality, and religious preferences.
15. Yes   No   Do not exchange business cards in the first interview.

Entrepreneurship Workbook

Name:_____ Date:_____ Period: _____

Critical Thinking

Many entrepreneurs become business owners by working their way up at an existing business. Think of an existing business where you might like to work. Research that business and complete the following.

1. Name of business _____
   _____

2. Address, phone number, and Web site address of business _____
   _____
   _____

3. How do you apply for a job at this business? _____
   _____
   _____

4. Are there any positions currently open? If so, what are they and what are the qualifications for these positions? If there are no positions available, list some that you might be interested in applying for if they were open. _____
   _____
   _____
   _____

5. Select one of the positions you listed in question 4. Imagine you have been asked to interview for this position. List at least five questions you could ask during the interview. _____
   _____
   _____
   _____

Chapter 14: Getting Started in Your Career

Name:_____ Date:_____ Period: _____

Multiple Choice

Circle the best response to each question.

1. If you were the owner of a business, which of the following behaviors would indicate you made a good hiring decision?
    A. The employee takes time off and calls in sick frequently.
    B. The employee does not follow the dress code.
    C. The employee takes initiative to learn new things.
    D. The employee arrives late and leaves early.

2. You just hired a new employee. Which of the following would result in that person making a bad impression on you and other employees?
    A. Arriving at work a little early the first few days.
    B. Dressing the part.
    C. Keeping negative opinions to him- or herself.
    D. Being passive and waiting for others to introduce themselves and show you how to complete job tasks.

3. Which of the following could have a negative effect on your work relationships?
    A. Complaining and making excuses.
    B. Being enthusiastic.
    C. Adapting to changes quickly.
    D. Pitching in and doing your part.

4. Which of the following is not a skill a business owner would value in his or her employees?
    A. Using active listening skills.
    B. Being aggressive and forcing others to agree with you.
    C. Compromising when necessary.
    D. Cooperating to meet the overall goals.

5. Which of the following is not suitable behavior in a performance review?
    A. Listening attentively to everything the other person says.
    B. Defending yourself instead of calmly accepting criticism.
    C. Taking notes about areas that need improvement.
    D. Asking questions so you fully understand what is expected of you.

6. Which of the following is not an effective way to earn a promotion?
    A. Join a professional organization.
    B. Propose new projects or suggest ways to improve productivity.
    C. Pass up opportunities for developing new skills.
    D. Meet with the business owner to discuss opportunities at the company.

Name:_____ Date:_____ Period:_____

True or False

Circle whether each statement is true or false.

1. True   False   For most people, education ends when they graduate from high school or college.
2. True   False   Although most business owners try to reward their employees with annual raises, they are not required to do so.
3. True   False   The only way to earn a promotion is if someone with more seniority leaves, enabling you to take over that job.
4. True   False   Business owners should stress the importance of building positive working relationships because they typically make employees more productive.
5. True   False   Whether you are the owner of a business or an employee, you should keep personal problems to yourself during the workday.

Fill in the Blank

Fill in the blank with a word from the box.

Employee handbook	**Performance review**	**Promoting**
Lifelong learning	**Probation**	**Retooling**
Mentor	**Professional development**	**Tuition reimbursement**

1. Business owners should provide employees with a(n) _____ that describes company policies and procedures.
2. During the _____ period, business owners can determine if an employee is right for the job.
3. Many business owners use a(n) _____ to evaluate their employees' performance in different areas.
4. Replacing old skills with new ones is referred to as _____.
5. _____ is a type of training in which you learn about new trends in your field or prepare for certification exams.

Name:_____ Date:_____ Period: _____

Short Answer

People who can work successfully as part of a team are valued in the work environment. Even entrepreneurs who work by themselves must be able to work with suppliers, customers, and others to be successful. Answer the questions below in the space provided.

1. Do you enjoy working in groups? Why or why not?

   _____
   _____
   _____
   _____
   _____
   _____

2. What do you think are the benefits of working in groups? Explain.

   _____
   _____
   _____
   _____
   _____
   _____

3. What do you think are the challenges of working in groups? Explain.

   _____
   _____
   _____
   _____
   _____
   _____

4. Frequently when working in groups, one person in the group takes over. What could you do to solve this problem?

   _____
   _____
   _____
   _____
   _____
   _____

5. Another common occurrence when working in groups is that one person in the group sits back and does nothing. What could you do to solve this problem?

   _____
   _____
   _____
   _____
   _____

6. If you were a business owner who managed a number of employee teams, what guidelines would you establish for the teams and team members?

   _____
   _____
   _____
   _____
   _____

7. Your textbook discusses performance reviews. Some businesses also use peer reviews. How would you feel about having your peers review your job performance? Explain.

   _____
   _____
   _____
   _____
   _____

Name: _____ Date: _____ Period: _____

Teamwork

Job satisfaction is important to everyone who works. The business owner can play a large role in keeping employees happy at work. Imagine you are the owner of a business and you have noticed your employees don't seem to be as happy at work as they once were. Working in small groups, discuss the following and record your answers below. Be prepared to share your ideas in class.

1. What things could cause workers to become dissatisfied with their jobs or workplace?

   _____
   _____
   _____
   _____
   _____

2. As the owner of the business, what would you do if you noticed your employees seemed unhappy or dissatisfied at work?

   _____
   _____
   _____
   _____
   _____

3. What would you do to try to raise the morale at your workplace?

   _____
   _____
   _____
   _____
   _____

Name:_____ Date:_____ Period: _____

Write Now

Imagine you own a company and you want to post a flyer around the office that summarizes general information for new employees and also lists the "Dos and Don'ts" for your workplace. Design your flyer in the space below.

Name:_____ Date:_____ Period: _____

Critical Thinking

1. Consider the following quote: "If you love what you do to earn a living, you never have to go to work." Do you think that is true? Explain your answer.

   _____
   _____
   _____
   _____
   _____
   _____
   _____
   _____
   _____

2. For older generations (those people who are your grandparents' age), it was common to stay in the same job for most of one's working life. Today, that happens less and less. Members of your generation are likely to have several different jobs (and even careers) during the course of their working life. The textbook refers to this as job jumping. Which do you think is better, to stay with one company or job all your working life or to work for several different companies or jobs? Explain your answer.

   _____
   _____
   _____
   _____
   _____
   _____
   _____
   _____
   _____

Entrepreneurship Workbook

Name:_____ Date:_____ Period: _____

Critical Thinking

Imagine you own an accounting business that employs 15 people. Explain why you have set the policies described below.

1. You are not allowed to make any personal calls or use your computer for personal business during the workday.

   _____
   _____
   _____
   _____
   _____

2. Visible tattoos and body piercings (other than in the ears) are prohibited.

   _____
   _____
   _____
   _____
   _____

3. Employees are required to do 20 hours of community service each year.

   _____
   _____
   _____
   _____
   _____

4. Employees are required to complete a certain amount of training and professional development each year.

   _____
   _____
   _____
   _____
   _____

Chapter 15: Being Productive in Your Career

Name: _____ Date: _____ Period: _____

Networking

Professional organizations provide many opportunities and benefits for an entrepreneur. Regardless of the type of business you own, you can benefit from the opportunities to meet other people in the industry. You can stay informed about current news and trends affecting your industry. And, you have access to classes, seminars, and other training opportunities sponsored by the organization. Think of a business you would like to own. Using the Internet, library, or other resources, research a professional organization for people in that type of business. Answer the questions below.

1. What is the name of the professional organization? Include the organization's Web site address.
   _____
   _____

2. How do you join the organization? Are there dues? If so, how much are they?
   _____
   _____

3. How can you participate in the organization? Does it have a local chapter? Does it have local, state, or regional meetings? If so, how often do the meetings take place?
   _____
   _____
   _____
   _____

4. What are the benefits of being a member of this organization?
   _____
   _____
   _____
   _____

5. Would you consider joining this organization? Explain your answer.
   _____
   _____
   _____
   _____

Entrepreneurship Workbook

Name:_____ Date:_____ Period: _____

Self-Evaluation

Time management is a critical skill for succeeding in business. Rate your time-management skills below. Use the following key to rate yourself.

1—That's me! 2—Describes me somewhat 3—Unsure 4—No way, not me!

_____ 1. I am always on time.

_____ 2. I frequently finish projects or assignments early.

_____ 3. I work best under pressure, so I wait until the last minute to do things.

_____ 4. I am easily overwhelmed when I have too much to do.

_____ 5. I like being organized and setting a schedule for myself.

_____ 6. I am usually late getting where I need to be.

_____ 7. I can't stand to be kept waiting by someone who is late.

_____ 8. Time really doesn't matter to me; I don't even wear a watch.

_____ 9. I like to be early when I need to be somewhere.

_____ 10. I always turn in assignments on time.

_____ 11. I like to juggle lots of things at one time.

_____ 12. I have a hard time telling people no when they ask for a favor, even if I really don't have time to help them.

_____ 13. I am not afraid to ask for help when I get overwhelmed.

_____ 14. I am good at setting goals and prioritizing what needs to be done.

_____ 15. I am a good time manager.

_____ 16. I can easily break larger projects down into more manageable or smaller chunks.

_____ 17. If I am running late, I always call ahead to let the person who is waiting on me know I will be a bit late.

_____ 18. I have a system that works for me to help me keep track of what I need to do.

_____ 19. I set realistic goals for myself.

_____ 20. I feel like I waste a lot of time.

Name:_____ Date:_____ Period:_____

Apply It

Sometimes we don't realize how we spend our time until we keep track of it. How do you spend your time on a typical day? Use the hourly planner below to record how you spend your time. Then, answer the questions that follow.

7 a.m.		**7 p.m.**	
8 a.m.		**8 p.m.**	
9 a.m.		**9 p.m.**	
10 a.m.		**10 p.m.**	
11 a.m.		**11 p.m.**	
Noon		**Midnight**	
1 p.m.		**1 a.m.**	
2 p.m.		**2 a.m.**	
3 p.m.		**3 a.m.**	
4 p.m.		**4 a.m.**	
5 p.m.		**5 a.m.**	
6 p.m.		**6 a.m.**	

1. What did you learn from this activity? _____
   _____
   _____

2. What surprised you the most about how you spend your time? _____
   _____
   _____

3. What can you do to make better use of your time? _____
   _____
   _____

Entrepreneurship Workbook

Name: _____ Date: _____ Period: _____

Problem Solver

As a business owner, your responsibilities include solving problems and managing workplace conflicts. Read each of the scenarios below. What would you do about each situation? Explain your answers.

1. You are working the cash register at the card shop you own and are busy helping a customer. Another customer asks for help. Your employee is talking to her good friend who stopped by the shop to chat and pretends she doesn't notice the other customer. What would you do?

   _____

   _____

   _____

   _____

2. One of your employees leaves early and asks a co-worker to complete his assigned tasks. The co-worker does not complain about the employee but she ends up working overtime that day. What would you do?

   _____

   _____

   _____

   _____

3. You overhear two employees talking badly about another co-worker. What should you do?

   _____

   _____

   _____

   _____

4. You own a toy store. A mother comes in with two young children. She leaves them to play in one of the aisles while she shops in another area of the store. The children are playing roughly and you see them break a toy. They try to hide it. What would you do?

   _____
   _____
   _____
   _____
   _____

5. Two female employees have complained to you about the attitude of a male co-worker. They say he is impatient toward them and makes negative comments about women in front of them. What would you do?

   _____
   _____
   _____
   _____
   _____

6. You own a fast food franchise. You notice that one of your hardest working employees sometimes slips free food and drinks to her friends who come in. What would you do?

   _____
   _____
   _____
   _____
   _____

Name:_____ Date:_____ Period: _____

Fill in the Blank

Complete each of the following statements with a term from the box.

Active	Passive	Punctual
Barriers	Peer pressure	Reliable
Criticism	Prejudice	Work ethics
Discrimination	Priorities	
Harassment	Professionalism	

1. Workplace _____ are anything that keeps employees from doing their job to the best of their ability.

2. _____ is unfair treatment of a person or group based on age, gender, race, religion, or disability.

3. Negative opinions that are not based on fact are referred to as _____.

4. _____ is unwanted, repeated behavior or communication that bothers, annoys, frightens, or stresses another person.

5. _____ is the ability to show respect to everyone around you while you perform your responsibilities as best as you can.

6. Beliefs and behaviors about what is right and wrong in a work environment are called _____.

7. When you set _____, you determine which tasks must be completed first.

8. Being _____ means that you are on time.

9. _____ occurs when someone influences your thoughts and actions.

10. Being an effective communicator means you use _____ listening to be sure you hear the response.

11. Employers expect workers to be _____, which means they can count on them to show up and do their work to the best of their ability.

116   Chapter 15

Name:_____ Date:_____ Period: _____

Check It

Business owners know how important it is to hire employees who are honest, dependable, and responsible. Place a check by the items below that demonstrate one or more of those qualities.

_____ 1. You respect the different backgrounds, cultures, and interests of other employees.

_____ 2. You deny responsibility for problems that arise and make sure the boss knows who to blame for them.

_____ 3. You show up every day on time.

_____ 4. You question the authority of supervisors and managers.

_____ 5. You take longer than allowed for breaks and lunches.

_____ 6. You call ahead if you are going to be late.

_____ 7. You refuse to work overtime to get the job done right.

_____ 8. You schedule days off well in advance.

_____ 9. You do not assist others if they need help so that you can get your own tasks done.

_____ 10. You take office supplies home for you and your family's personal use.

_____ 11. You take care of personal business on your own time.

_____ 12. You show patience with others who are not able to work as fast as you.

_____ 13. You leave work early to play golf with your co-workers.

_____ 14. You join a professional organization so that you can meet other people in your industry.

_____ 15. You convince your co-workers to work overtime to finish an important project ahead of schedule.

_____ 16. You accept a cash gift from a vendor from whom you bought office supplies.

_____ 17. You request training on a new piece of equipment.

_____ 18. You participate in your company's safety committee.

_____ 19. You do not report that a new employee does not know how to use the equipment.

_____ 20. You ask other employees probing questions about their personal lives.

Name:_____ Date:_____ Period: _____

Matching

Match the term in the right column to its definition.

_____ 1. Requires all employers to provide a safe and healthful workplace.

_____ 2. Prohibits employers from paying workers less simply because of their gender.

_____ 3. States that employers may not use race, skin color, religion, sex, or national origin as a reason to promote, not promote, hire, or fire an employee.

_____ 4. Provides certain employees with up to 12 weeks of unpaid, job-protected leave per year.

_____ 5. Federal agency responsible for investigating charges of discrimination against employers.

_____ 6. Organization whose purpose is to improve wages and working conditions for workers.

_____ 7. Association of people who are all employed in the same field or industry.

_____ 8. Agency that was formed to inspect companies and enforce safety laws.

A. Professional association

B. Equal Employment Opportunity Commission (EEOC)

C. Occupational Safety and Health Administration (OSHA)

D. Occupational Safety and Health Act

E. Family and Medical Leave Act (FMLA)

F. Trade union

G. Equal Pay Act of 1963

H. Civil Rights Act of 1964

Chapter 16: Living a Healthy and Balanced Life

Name:_____ Date:_____ Period: _____

Check It

Running your own business can be challenging and even stressful at times. Read the statements below. Place a check beside the items that show how to balance work with your personal life.

_____ 1. I get regular exercise, even if it means putting off something for work until a later time.

_____ 2. I do not talk about my feelings with other people.

_____ 3. I avoid leisure activities so that I can focus on the operations of my business and look for ways to expand it.

_____ 4. I commit time every week to my personal interests and hobbies.

_____ 5. I am not active in the community because it is a drain on my energy and my financial resources.

_____ 6. I avoid reading newspapers, news magazines, and Web sites because they never publish information about my company.

_____ 7. I keep up with legislation and laws that affect my business.

_____ 8. I am involved with my community because I meet new people who often become new customers.

_____ 9. I do not pay taxes because I do not use city services.

_____ 10. I discourage my employees from participating in volunteer activities because it usually means they have less time to work for me.

_____ 11. I promote the use of recycling programs at my company and use recycled paper and plastics whenever possible.

_____ 12. I prioritize my responsibilities to help me stay organized.

_____ 13. I deal with stress by going to the local drive-thru and eating lots of junk food.

_____ 14. I avoid risky behaviors, such as smoking and drinking.

_____ 15. I eat regular meals with my family and take my time eating.

Name:_____ Date:_____ Period: _____

True or False

Circle whether each statement is true or false.

1. True   False   Relationships are important in every role of your life and at every stage of your life.
2. True   False   Relationships are not as important to entrepreneurs because they usually work by themselves.
3. True   False   The best solution to a dysfunctional relationship is to walk away and end it.
4. True   False   The qualities of a healthy relationship are much the same whether it is with a close friend, colleague, or business associate.
5. True   False   Healthy relationships contribute to all areas of your wellness, including your physical and intellectual wellness.
6. True   False   The type of business you choose to start will not affect your lifestyle.
7. True   False   Leisure activities can improve your personal well-being by helping you develop new skills and interests.
8. True   False   Balancing work and family is only a women's issue.
9. True   False   People must live physically near each other or in the same neighborhood to be a community.
10. True   False   Part of lifelong learning is keeping up with current events and being aware of changes around you.
11. True   False   Being involved in your community can lead to increased opportunities and higher self-esteem.
12. True   False   Although voting demonstrates civic responsibility, you are not required by law to do it.
13. True   False   Because you do not get paid for volunteering, it is not an effective way to gain work experience.
14. True   False   Driving a car instead of walking is a good example of how to preserve the environment.
15. True   False   Having supportive friends and family members contributes to your emotional health.

Name:_____ Date:_____ Period: _____

Critical Thinking

Think of a business you would like to start. Describe the roles you could take on in each of the following areas of your life to help prepare you to run that business.

1. **Family.** _____
   _____
   _____
   _____

2. **School.** _____
   _____
   _____
   _____

3. **Peers.** _____
   _____
   _____
   _____

4. **Community.** _____
   _____
   _____
   _____

5. **Work.** _____
   _____
   _____
   _____

Entrepreneurship Workbook

Name:_____ Date:_____ Period: _____

Write Now

Even business owners need to relax and have fun sometimes. Leisure activities help energize and refresh you and focus your thoughts on people and things outside of work. Through leisure activities, you can develop skills and abilities. You can also acquire knowledge through new experiences that can help you be more productive in all areas of your life. List the things you do for fun or in your leisure time. Then write a sentence about how the activity can help you build and strengthen your workplace skills.

Leisure Activity	How It Strengthens My Workplace Skills

Name:_____ Date:_____ Period: _____

Write Now

Planning for the future is important. Regardless of the type of business you'd like to own or the career path you want to pursue, it's never too early to start planning. Think about each of the following questions and record your answers.

1. What do you plan to do when you graduate from high school?

   _____
   _____
   _____
   _____

2. What type of business would you like to own in the future?

   _____
   _____
   _____
   _____

3. Where do you think you will be living in 10 years? Include both the location and type of housing.

   _____
   _____
   _____
   _____

4. What will your family life be like?

   _____
   _____
   _____
   _____

Name:_____ Date:_____ Period: _____

Short Answer

Answer the questions below about lifelong learning.

1. What is lifelong learning?

   _____
   _____
   _____
   _____

2. Do you think lifelong learning is important? Explain.

   _____
   _____
   _____
   _____

3. Think of older adults you know. What types of lifelong learning are they involved in?

   _____
   _____
   _____
   _____

4. If you could take a class in anything you wanted today, what would it be and why?

   _____
   _____
   _____
   _____

5. What types of lifelong learning would benefit an entrepreneur? Explain your answer.

   _____
   _____
   _____
   _____

Name:_____ Date:_____ Period: _____

Self-Evaluation

Rate your health and wellness habits. Use the following key to rate yourself:

1—That's me!   2—Describes me somewhat   3—Unsure   4—No way, not me!

_____ 1. I eat a healthy breakfast regularly.

_____ 2. I exercise regularly.

_____ 3. I drink plenty of water.

_____ 4. I eat a balanced diet.

_____ 5. I eat a lot of junk food.

_____ 6. I always wear a seat belt.

_____ 7. I maintain a healthy weight.

_____ 8. I avoid exercise at all costs.

_____ 9. I have lots of energy and like to be active.

_____ 10. I have a supportive family.

_____ 11. I have hobbies or leisure activities I enjoy.

_____ 12. I have healthy friendships.

_____ 13. I limit the fats in my diet.

_____ 14. I have a huge sweet tooth.

_____ 15. I enjoy school and learning.

_____ 16. I usually get enough rest.

_____ 17. I avoid risky behavior.

_____ 18. Living a healthy lifestyle is important to me.

_____ 19. I am a picky eater.

_____ 20. I am generally a happy person.

_____ 21. I set realistic goals for myself.

_____ 22. I deal with stress in healthy ways.

_____ 23. I generally have a positive attitude.

Chapter 17: Starting Your Own Business

Name:_____ Date:_____ Period: _____

Matching

Classify the following list according to the *major* type of business in which the organization is involved. Use the key on the right.

____ 1. Wal-Mart

____ 2. General Electric

____ 3. JC Penney

____ 4. Hallmark Gold Crown Stores

____ 5. D&R Shoe Repair

____ 6. Goodyear Tire & Rubber Company

____ 7. ABC Childcare Center

____ 8. Costco Wholesale Corporation

____ 9. eBay

____ 10. Sam's Club

____ 11. Sandy & Smith Tailoring

____ 12. Barbara's Fudge & Candies

____ 13. Caterpillar Inc.

____ 14. H&R Block Tax Professionals

____ 15. Salvation Army

____ 16. Bettina's Hair & Nails

____ 17. Three Guys and a Truck Movers

____ 18. Pepsi Bottling Group Inc.

____ 19. T-shirts for Today.com

____ 20. Goodwill Industries

E = E-commerce
M = Manufacturing
N = Nonprofit
R = Retailing
S = Service
W = Wholesaling

Name:_____ Date:_____ Period: _____

Fill in the Blank

Complete each statement with a term from the box.

Board of directors	Limited liability
Cooperative	Nonprofit
Corporation	Partnership
Dividend	Share
Liability	Sole proprietorship

1. In a(n) _____, at least two individuals share the management, profit, and liability for the business.
2. A(n) _____ is a business that is owned by a single individual.
3. _____ is the legal obligation of a business owner to use personal money and possessions to pay business debt.
4. In a(n) _____ company, the business owners cannot be legally forced to use personal money and possessions to pay business debt.
5. In a(n) _____, the business is considered an entity under the law and the owner or owners have limited liability.
6. A(n) _____ corporation operates to serve the good of society rather than to provide profits to shareholders.
7. Most states require a corporation to have a(n) _____, which consists of one or more persons responsible for making decisions about how the business should be run.
8. A unit of ownership in a corporation is called a(n) _____.
9. Some corporations pay a(n) _____ to shareholders, which is a portion of the corporation's profit.
10. A(n) _____ is a business owned, controlled, and operated for the mutual benefit of its members.

Name:_____ Date:_____ Period: _____

Multiple Choice

Select the best response to the statements below.

1. A type of business that takes materials and builds goods that it can sell to others is a

   A. manufacturer.

   B. nonprofit corporation.

   C. franchise.

   D. service provider.

2. A type of business that is also known as the middleman or intermediary is a(n)

   A. e-commerce company.

   B. franchise.

   C. manufacturer.

   D. wholesaler.

3. Wholesalers and retailers are commonly referred to as

   A. franchises.

   B. trade businesses.

   C. trade agreements.

   D. cooperatives.

4. A type of business that takes resources from the environment and converts them into a form that can be sold to manufacturers is a(n)

   A. farming business.

   B. extraction business.

   C. retailer.

   D. wholesaler.

5. A type of business that earns money through donations, government grants, or the sale of goods and services is a

   A. nonprofit corporation.

   B. sole proprietorship.

   C. cooperative.

   D. subchapter S corporation.

6. A type of business in which an established company sells the right for others to use the company's name and operating plan to sell products or services is a(n)

   A. franchise.

   B. farming business.

   C. e-commerce business.

   D. nonprofit corporation.

7. A type of business that buys goods and then sells them directly to consumers is a(n)

   A. manufacturer.

   B. extraction business.

   C. retailer.

   D. wholesaler.

Name: _____ Date: _____ Period: _____

Critical Thinking

Complete the following table. In the first column, list your hobbies, interests, and skills. In the middle column, list businesses you could start using your unique knowledge and your hobbies, interests, and skills. In the third column, identify the type for each business.

Hobbies, Interests, and Skills	Businesses You Could Start	Business Type: Manufacturing, Retail, Service, or Wholesale

Choose one of your business ideas and come up with a name for it. Explain why you chose that business.

_____

_____

_____

_____

Entrepreneurship Workbook

Name:_____ Date:_____ Period: _____

Teamwork

Working with a partner, imagine you are entrepreneurs looking for a business to start. Read each of the scenarios below, and think of a business you could launch.

1. A business needed in your community _____
   _____

2. A business you could run while working part-time _____
   _____

3. An online business _____
   _____

4. A business that could be started with $100 _____
   _____

5. A business that you can franchise _____
   _____

6. A service business _____
   _____

7. A partnership between you and someone else _____
   _____

8. A business whose customers are kids between the ages of 8 and 12 _____
   _____

9. A business that relates to the environment _____
   _____

10. A business that you think will fail (you might be surprised) _____
    _____

Name:_____ Date:_____ Period: _____

Critical Thinking

Pick four businesses you go to as a customer. For each one, think of a competing business you could start. Describe how you would make your business better.

Business: _____	**Business:** _____
Business: _____	**Business:** _____

Name:_____ Date:_____ Period: _____

Crossword

Across:
4. Business owned by a single individual
5. Earnings greater than the businesses expenses, or money leftover when bills are paid
7. Measurement unit equal to the amount of work one employee performs in one hour
9. Arrangement in which an established company sells the right for others to use the company's name and operating plan to sell products or services
10. Business owned, controlled, and operated for the mutual benefit of its members
11. Business that stores Web site information on its server computers
12. Legal obligation of an owner to use personal money and possessions to pay business debt

Down:
1. Business that is considered a type of person or entity under the law
2. Portion of the company's profit paid to shareholders
3. Goods bought by the public
6. Goods sold to other manufacturing businesses
8. Partnership in which all partners have unlimited liability

Possible Answers:

consumer, cooperative, corporation, dividend, franchise, general, industrial, liability, man-hour, profit, sole proprietorship, Web host

Chapter 18: Planning Your Own Business

Name:_____ Date:_____ Period: _____

Matching

Match the part of the business plan with its description.

____ 1. Part that describes how the business will be managed, focusing on production, distribution, operations, purchasing, and inventory.

____ 2. Part that describes your plans to expand and grow the business and the challenges you could face.

____ 3. Part that describes the way the management of the company will be set up, including profiles of managers and information about training and motivating employees.

____ 4. Part in which you summarize the key concepts of the business, including its mission statement, name and location, products or services, owner's name and function, and future plans.

____ 5. Part that shows projected figures, such as estimated sales and expenses, for five years as well as the type of loans or other arrangements you want to use to fund the business.

____ 6. Part that describes the product or service, discusses the type of business you will start, and explains the type of business ownership you will use.

____ 7. Part that describes how and why your product or service will sell; includes the size of the market, its trends and characteristics, and its growth rate.

____ 8. Part that describes the legal ownership of the business, how it will be protected by insurance, and any relevant government regulations that affect it.

A. Business idea
B. Business management
C. Executive summary
D. Financial strategies
E. Legal structures
F. Opportunity and market analysis
G. Organizational structures
H. Plan for growth

Name:_____ Date:_____ Period: _____

Fill in the Blank

Complete each sentence with the correct term from the box.

Buying patterns	Geography	Place
Competition	Indirect competitors	Price
Demographics	Market research	Promotion
Direct competitors	Marketing plan	Psychology
Focus group	People	Target market

1. A(n) _____ is a detailed guide that identifies your goals and strategies for selling your product or service to as many customers as possible.

2. The other companies that are in business to sell to the same customers as you are referred to as the _____.

3. _____ are businesses that sell a product or service similar to yours.

4. _____ are businesses that sell different products or services than yours but fill the same need or want.

5. The strategy area in a marketing plan that refers to the way you make the product or service available to your customers is called _____.

6. The strategy area in a marketing plan that refers to the steps you take to convince customers to buy your product or service is called _____.

7. Through _____, you gain an understanding of potential customers, the competition, and the current business environment.

8. A customer profile includes information on _____, such as the age, gender, education, and ethnic background of customers.

9. By examining consumer _____, you learn how often your customers shop, when they shop, and where they shop.

10. One method for gathering market research is to run a(n) _____, which is a discussion among a small number of people.

Name:_____ Date:_____ Period: _____

Creating a Business Plan

Think of a business you would like to start. Use the following template to create your business plan. Note that some of the items you will have to complete in the business plan are discussed in later chapters of your text.

1. Describe your business idea.

   _____
   _____
   _____
   _____
   _____
   _____
   _____
   _____
   _____

2. What is the name of your business?

   _____

3. Explain how your idea will satisfy a consumer need.

   _____
   _____
   _____

4. Provide contact information for each owner.

   _____
   _____
   _____

5. If there is more than one owner, describe how the business ownership will be shared. (Refer to the types of business ownership discussed in Chapter 17.)

   _____
   _____
   _____

Entrepreneurship Workbook

Name:_____ Date:_____ Period: _____

Economics of One Unit

1. What type of business are you starting?

   _____

   _____

   _____

2. Identify your unit of sale. In general, units of sale are defined by the type of business. For example, retailers use one unit or item; manufacturers use one order; service businesses use one hour of service or another standard block of time; and wholesalers use one dozen of the unit or item.

   _____

3. Calculate the economics of one unit. This is a calculation that determines the profit or loss that a business earns every time a customer buys a unit of sale. It is discussed in Chapter 24 of the text. To calculate the economics of one unit, subtract the **Cost of Goods Sold per Unit** from the **Selling Price per Unit**.

Manufacturing Business: unit = _____

Selling Price per Unit: $ _____

    Labor Cost per Hour: $ _____

    No. of Hours per Unit: + $ _____ → $ _____

    Cost of Materials per Unit: + $ _____

Cost of Goods Sold per Unit: $ _____ → $ _____

Gross Profit per Unit: $ _____

Wholesale Business: unit = _____

Selling Price per Unit: $ _____

Cost of Goods Sold per Unit: $ _____

Gross Profit per Unit: $ _____

Retail Business: unit = _____

Selling Price per Unit: $ _____
Cost of Goods Sold per Unit: $ _____
Gross Profit per Unit: $ _____

Service Business: unit = _____

Selling Price per Unit: $ _____
    Supplies per unit: $ _____
    Labor Cost per Hour: + $ _____
Cost of Goods Sold per Unit: $ _____ → $ _____
Gross Profit per Unit: $ _____

Name:_____ Date:_____ Period: _____

Return on Investment

Business Goals

1. What is your short-term business goal (less than one year)? What do you plan to invest to achieve this goal? What is your expected return on investment (ROI)? (Note that ROI is discussed in Chapter 21 of your text.)

   _____
   _____
   _____

2. What is your long-term business goal (from one to five years)? What do you plan to invest to achieve this goal? What is your expected ROI?

   _____
   _____
   _____

Personal Goals

3. What are your long-term personal and career goals?

   Personal _____
   _____
   _____
   _____

   Career _____
   _____
   _____
   _____

4. How much education will you need for your career?

   _____
   _____

5. Have you tried to get a part-time job related to your chosen career?

   _____
   _____

Name:_____ Date:_____ Period: _____

Opportunity Recognition

1. What resources and skills do you (and the other owners of your business) have that will help make your business successful?

   _____
   _____
   _____

2. Perform a SWOT analysis of your business. Type of business:

   Strengths (Your abilities and contacts):

   _____
   _____
   _____

   Weaknesses (Problems you face, from lack of money or training to lack of time or experience):

   _____
   _____
   _____

   Opportunities (Lucky breaks or creative advantages you can use to get ahead of the competition):

   _____
   _____
   _____

   Threats (Anything that might be bad for the business, from competitors to legal problems):

   _____
   _____
   _____

Name:_____ Date:_____ Period: _____

Core Beliefs

1. Describe three core beliefs you will use in running your company.
   _____
   _____
   _____

2. Choose a motto (short saying that expresses the core principles) for your company.
   _____
   _____
   _____

Supply and Demand

1. What factors will influence the demand for your product or service?
   _____
   _____
   _____

2. What factors will influence the supply for your product or service?
   _____
   _____
   _____

Name:_____ Date:_____ Period: _____

Competitive Advantage

1. What is your competitive advantage?

Competitive Advantage	Yes/No	Description
Quality		
Price		
Location		
Selection		
Service		
Speed		
Reputation		

2. Who are your primary competitors? Where are they located?

   _____
   _____
   _____

3. How will your business help others? List all organizations to which you plan to contribute. (Your contribution may be time, money, your product or service, or something else.)

   _____
   _____
   _____

Entrepreneurship Workbook

Name:_____ Date:_____ Period: _____

Operating Costs

1. List and estimate your monthly fixed costs and your monthly variable costs.

Fixed Costs	Estimate	Variable Costs	Estimate

2. Recalculate your economics of one unit, allocating as many variable costs as possible.

Selling Price per Unit: $ _____

    Supplies/Materials: $ _____

    Labor: + $ _____

Cost of Goods Sold per Unit: $ _____ $ _____

    Commission: $ _____

    Packaging: + $ _____

    Total Other Variable Cost per Unit: $ _____ $ _____

Total Variable Cost per Unit: $ _____ $ _____

Gross Profit per Unit: $ _____

Name:_____ Date:_____ Period: _____

Marketing

1. Describe the Five Ps for your business:

   People—Who will your customers be?

   _____
   _____
   _____

   Product—Why will your product or service meet a consumer need?

   _____
   _____
   _____

   Place—Where do you intend to sell your product or service?

   _____
   _____
   _____

   Price—What price do you plan to sell your product or service for, and why?

   _____
   _____
   _____

   Promotion—How do you plan to advertise and promote your product?

   _____
   _____
   _____

2. Fill out a marketing plan for your business.

Methods	Description	Target Market	Amount to Be Spent
Brochures			
Business Cards			
Flyers			
Promo Items			
Special Events			
E-mail			

3. Do you intend to publicize your philanthropy (charitable activities)? Why or why not? If you do, explain how you will work your philanthropy into your marketing.

___
___
___
___
___
___

Name:_____ Date:_____ Period: _____

Market Research

1. Describe your target market.

   _____
   _____
   _____
   _____
   _____
   _____

2. Brainstorm five market research questions.

   _____
   _____
   _____
   _____
   _____
   _____
   _____

Record Keeping

1. Describe your record-keeping system.

   _____
   _____
   _____
   _____
   _____
   _____

2. List all bank accounts you will open for your business.

   _____
   _____
   _____
   _____
   _____
   _____

Name:_____ Date:_____ Period: _____

Projected Income Statement

1. Complete a monthly projected budget and one-year income statement for your business.

	Jan	Feb	Mar	Apr	May	June	July	Aug	Sept	Oct	Nov	Dec	Total
Units sold*													
Unit selling price*													
Sales/Revenue													
Total Cost of Goods Sold													
Total Other Variable Costs													
Total Variable Costs													
Gross Profit													
Total Fixed Costs													
Profit													

Less Taxes (25%) [ ]
Net Profit [ ]

- Total Sales/Revenue = Units Sold × Unit Selling Price
- Total Cost of Goods or Services Sold = Units Sold × Cost of Goods or Services Sold per Unit
- Total Other Variable Costs = Units Sold × Other Variable Costs per Unit
- Total Variable Costs = Total Cost of Goods or Services Sold + Total Other Variable Costs
- Gross Profit = Total Sales − Total Variable Costs
- Total Fixed Costs = Total of USAIIRDO**
- Profit/(Loss) = Gross Profit − Total Variable Costs
- Taxes = Profit × .25 (estimated)
- Net Profit = Profit − Taxes

* *Units Sold* and *Unit Selling Price* are not part of the Income Statement, but when multiplied together give *Total Sales/Revenue*.

** Utilities, Salaries, Advertising, Insurance, Interest, Rent, Depreciation, Other

2. Use your projected one-year income statement to calculate:

   Projected ROI for one year: _____ %; Projected ROS for one year: _____ %

Financing Strategy

1. What legal structure have you chosen for your business? Why?

   _____
   _____
   _____
   _____
   _____

2. List and total the cost of items you will need to buy to start your business.

Item	Quantity	Cost per Item	Total
Add a cash reserve of three months' fixed costs			
Estimated Total Start-Up Costs			

Entrepreneurship Workbook

3. List the sources of financing for your start-up capital. Identify whether each source is equity, debt, or a gift. Indicate the amount and type for each source. (Note that financing is discussed in Chapter 19 of your text.)

Source	Equity	Debt	Gift	Total
Personal Savings				
Relatives				
Friends				
Investors				
Grants				
Other				
Total				$

4. What is your debt ratio? What is your debt-to-equity ratio?

_____
_____
_____
_____

5. What is your payback period? In other words, how long will it take you to earn enough profit to cover start-up capital?

_____
_____
_____
_____

Name:_____ Date:_____ Period: _____

Negotiation

Describe any suppliers with whom you will have to negotiate.

_____
_____
_____

Buying Wholesale

1. Where will you purchase the products you plan to sell, or the products you plan to use to manufacture the products you will be selling?

Name of Supplier	Item	Price

2. Have you applied for a sales tax ID number?

_____
_____

Entrepreneurship Workbook

Chapter 19: Managing Your Business

Name:_____ Date:_____ Period: _____

Fill in the Blank

Complete each statement with the correct term from the box.

Barter	**Debt**	**SBICs**
Bootstrapping	**Equity**	**Start-up**
Business associate	**Financing**	**Venture capitalists**
Cash reserves	**Partners**	
Credit limit	**Payback**	

1. Raising money for a business is called _____.

2. _____ investment is the one-time sum required to launch a business and cover the start-up expenses.

3. An entrepreneur who starts a business without any outside help is _____.

4. A(n) _____ is the maximum amount you can charge to a credit card.

5. _____ are companies that invest in businesses.

6. _____ are people who assume a percentage of the ownership of a business in exchange for equity financing.

7. _____ financing is a type of loan provided by other companies with which you do business.

8. _____ financing is the trading of items or services between businesses, allowing both businesses to get what they want without spending any money.

9. _____ financing is the selling of shares or ownership in the business to sources such as relatives, friends, venture capitalists, or partners.

10. _____ financing means borrowing money from a source such as a bank, credit union, relative, or friend.

11. _____ is the amount of time it takes a business to earn enough in profit to cover the start-up investment.

12. The money a business sets aside for emergencies is its _____.

Name:_____ Date:_____ Period: _____

Thumb Up! Thumbs Down!

Raising money to start a business can be challenging. There are several options available. Each one has advantages and disadvantages. For each of the ways listed below, describe the advantages in the Thumbs Up box and the disadvantages in the Thumbs Down box.

1. Debt financing through a bank or credit union

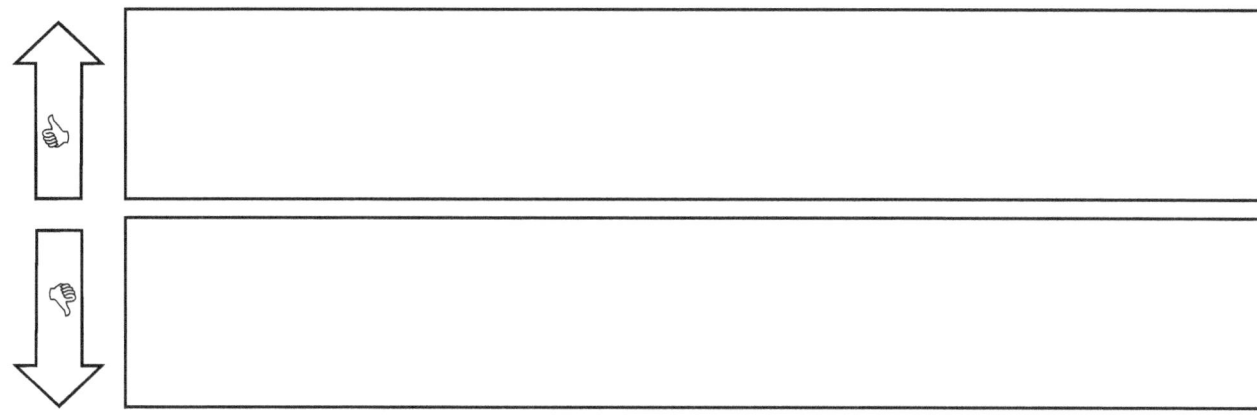

2. Debt financing through a relative or friend

Entrepreneurship Workbook

3. Equity financing from a relative or friend

   👍 [   ]

   👎 [   ]

4. Equity financing through a partner

   👍 [   ]

   👎 [   ]

5. Equity financing through an angel investor

   👍 [   ]

   👎 [   ]

Which source of financing would you use to start up your own business? Explain why.

_____
_____
_____
_____

Name:_____ Date:_____ Period: _____

Critical Thinking

The textbook discusses three basic styles of leadership. In the space below, briefly describe each style. Explain the advantages and disadvantages of each style and list examples of people you have seen demonstrate this style of leadership.

1. Authoritarian

   _____
   _____
   _____

2. Democratic

   _____
   _____
   _____

3. Delegating

   _____
   _____
   _____

4. If you owned your own business, which style of leadership would you most likely use? Why?

   _____
   _____
   _____

5. Which style of leadership would you most like to work under? Why?

   _____
   _____
   _____

Name:_____ Date:_____ Period: _____

Managing Your Business

As a small business grows and expands, the owner might find it necessary to set up departments to handle tasks and responsibilities. Some typical business departments are listed in the table below. Write a description of each department's function.

Department	Function
Accounting	
Production	
Sales	
Administration	
Customer Service	
Human Resources	
Research and Development	
Advertising	
Shipping and Receiving	
Quality Control	

Name:_____ Date:_____ Period: _____

Sequence

The five basic steps in the selling process are listed below, but they are not in the correct order. Write which number in the process each step represents.

_____ **Preparing for a sales call.** A sales call is direct contact between the sales person and the customer. It is the sales person's opportunity to present the product to the customer. It could be a phone call, a meeting, or an e-mail exchange. To prepare for a sales call, a sales person first sets up an appointment. He or she then spends time learning about the prospect, learning about the product or service to sell, developing a sales strategy, and writing a presentation outline.

_____ **Closing a sale.** Closing a sale means obtaining a commitment, which is an agreement from the customer to buy. Technically, the final closing occurs when the customer accepts delivery of the product or service and payment is received.

_____ **Making the sales call.** Keys to a successful sales call include being on time, using effective communication skills to build trust and respect with the customer, asking questions and taking notes, and responding truthfully to all customer objections.

_____ **Finding and qualifying sales leads.** A sales lead is a person or company that has some characteristics of your target market and might become a potential customer. Salespeople evaluate, or qualify, the lead to determine the likelihood that it will become a prospect. That way, they can avoid wasting time pursuing leads that are unlikely to result in a sale.

_____ **Following up.** A successful sales person always follows up a sale by contacting the customer to make sure he or she is satisfied. A happy customer leads to a good relationship and additional sales.

Check It

Place a check beside those of the following characteristics and behaviors that contribute to successful selling.

_____ 1. Dependability _____ 5. Persistence _____ 8. Indifferent

_____ 2. Talking constantly _____ 6. Intolerance _____ 9. Honest

_____ 3. Fidgeting and looking around the room _____ 7. Good listening skills _____ 10. Nervous and timid

_____ 4. Positive attitude

Explain why you selected certain characteristics over others.

_____
_____
_____

Entrepreneurship Workbook

Name:_____ Date:_____ Period: _____

Apply It

Refer to the business plan you created in the Chapter 17 activities. In the space below, create an organizational chart for your business. If you did not complete the business plan, think of a business or school or community group that you would like to start. Create an organizational chart for it.

Chapter 20: Personal Money Management

Name:_____ Date:_____ Period:_____

Teamwork

Working in small groups, imagine you are starting the following companies. Identify whether each item listed is something you need (**N**) or something you want (**W**) in order to run the business.

Lemonade Stand

_____ Lemonade mix

_____ Water

_____ Glass Pitchers

_____ Plastic Pitchers

_____ Cups

_____ Fancy stir sticks

_____ Professionally designed sign to hang at the stand

_____ Fresh lemons, limes, strawberries, and cherries for garnish

_____ Canopy, benches, and decorations for customer seating

_____ Table for preparing and serving lemonade

_____ Matching aprons for workers

_____ Fans to keep serving area cool

Lawn Care Service

_____ Lawnmower

_____ Business cards for each worker

_____ Rakes

_____ Matching shirts and caps for workers

_____ Full-color promotional brochures

_____ Pruning shears

_____ New truck for each worker

_____ Trimmer/edger

Painting Company

_____ Ladders

_____ Interior designer on staff

_____ Paintbrushes and rollers

_____ Overalls and company shirts for all workers

_____ Professionally designed Web site

_____ Paint thinner and cleaning solution

_____ Paint scrapers and sandpaper

_____ Paint trays

_____ Laptop or portable computer for each worker

_____ Radio and CD player

Entrepreneurship Workbook 157

Name:_____ Date:_____ Period: _____

Financial Self-Evaluation

Money management is a critical skill for succeeding in business. Rate your money management skills below. Use the following key to rate yourself.

1—That's me!   2—Describes me somewhat   3—Unsure   4—No way, not me!

_____ 1. I believe it is important to save money.

_____ 2. When I see something I want, I should buy it, regardless of how much it costs.

_____ 3. Money burns a hole in my pocket.

_____ 4. I believe you should only pay cash when buying things.

_____ 5. I am good at making money.

_____ 6. As soon as I am old enough, I plan to get a credit card.

_____ 7. I budget my money wisely.

_____ 8. I spend a lot of time thinking about a purchase before I make the purchase.

_____ 9. I often cannot account for how I spent my money.

_____ 10. It is important to make charitable contributions.

_____ 11. I often ask my parents for an advance on my allowance to buy something I want.

_____ 12. I am able save money to buy something I really want, even if it takes a considerable amount of time.

_____ 13. I gladly loan money to my friends.

_____ 14. If I see something I want, I wait until it is on sale to buy it.

_____ 15. I am happy to buy used items to save money.

Circle the items that you rated with a "1." What do you think these items say about your money management skills?

_____
_____
_____
_____

158   Chapter 20

Name:_____ Date:_____ Period: _____

Key Terms

Imagine you are the owner of a business. You must explain the concept of budgeting to your employees. Use each term below in a sentence that would help the employees understand what it means.

1. Budget _____
   _____

2. Income _____
   _____

3. Expenses _____
   _____

4. Variable income _____
   _____

5. Fixed expenses _____
   _____

6. Estimate _____
   _____

7. Surplus _____
   _____

8. Deficit _____
   _____

Entrepreneurship Workbook

Name:_____ Date:_____ Period: _____

Budgeting

Imagine you run a housecleaning business. Below is a sample monthly budget. Review the budget, and then answer the questions that follow.

	Actual	Estimated
Income		
Wages	$475.00	
Tips		$120.00
Subtotal	**$475.00**	**$120.00**
Total Income		
Expenses		
Disinfectant	$22.00	
Scouring powder	$11.00	
Furniture polish	$8.00	
Window cleaner	$12.00	
Rubber gloves	$9.00	
Paper towels	$15.00	
Sponges	$14.00	
Advertising		$35.00
Transportation		$43.00
Phone		$25.00
Administrative Costs (invoicing, postage, etc.)		$18.00
Miscellaneous		$25.00
Subtotal	**$91.00**	**$146.00**
Total Expenses		

What is the total income? Show your work in the space below.

_____
_____
_____

What are the total expenses? Show your work in the space below.

_____
_____
_____

Is it a surplus or a deficit? What is the amount of the surplus or deficit? Show your work in the space below.

_____
_____
_____

Budgeting

Imagine you are going to college after you graduate and you want to start budgeting now. Research a university or college you would like to attend. You can visit its Web site or get information by calling the university. You might also ask your school guidance counselor about information for the university. Find out the following costs for one year.

1. Tuition _____
2. Housing _____
3. Meal plans _____
4. Textbooks _____
5. Other fees _____
6. Miscellaneous costs _____
7. What are the total costs for one year? Show your work in the space below.

   _____
   _____

8. What expenses or costs could be reduced? Explain how they could be reduced.

   _____
   _____
   _____

Entrepreneurship Workbook

Name:_____ Date:_____ Period: _____

Apply It

Keep track of your spending for one week. Include what you bought, how much it cost, where you got the money, and if you are happy with your purchase.

Item you purchased	How much did it cost?	Where did you get the money?	Are you satisfied with your purchase?

1. How did you spend the majority of your money?
   _____
   _____

2. Were you satisfied with the majority of your purchases? Explain.
   _____
   _____

3. What choices did you have to make concerning your purchases during the week? Explain.
   _____
   _____

Name: _____ Date: _____ Period: _____

Critical Thinking

An important consideration in managing your business's money is choosing the most appropriate method of payment. Should you pay your employees with cash or a check? Should you buy supplies using a credit card or a debit card? Complete the table below on the different methods of payment.

Payment Method	Benefits	Drawbacks
Cash		
Check		
Debit card		
Credit card		

Entrepreneurship Workbook

Chapter 21: Personal Financial Planning

Name:_____ Date:_____ Period: _____

Multiple Choice

Select the best response to each question.

1. At which type of bank would a business most likely open its checking account?

    A. Commercial bank

    B. Central bank

    C. Credit union

    D. None of the above

2. Which type of bank account enables you to access your money and pay for things using a check or debit card?

    A. Investment account

    B. Small business loan

    C. Checking account

    D. Savings account

3. Which of the following is an effective way to manage your bank account?

    A. Wait until your bank statement comes to enter your transactions in your account register.

    B. Keep records of every transaction you make.

    C. Shred or throw out any ATM receipts as soon as the transaction is complete.

    D. All of the above.

4. What is the biggest difference between saving and investing?

    A. Investing is riskier than saving because the deposit is usually not insured and your return on investment is not guaranteed.

    B. You cannot earn money through saving.

    C. You do not have to use your own money when you invest.

    D. You cannot withdraw money you have invested.

5. Which type of account requires you to leave money you have deposited untouched for a set amount of time?

    A. Checking account

    B. Passbook savings account

    C. Money market account

    D. Time account

6. Which type of investment represents stock ownership in a company?

    A. Fixed income

    B. Equity

    C. Commodity

    D. Portfolio

7. Which type of tax-deferred investment option might a business offer its employees?

    A. Social Security

    B. Passbook savings account

    C. 401(k) savings plan

    D. Mutual fund

8. Which of the following could provide an entrepreneur with the money he or she needs to start up a new business?

    A. Social Security

    B. Individual Retirement Account

    C. Business plan

    D. Loan

9. If you borrowed money from a friend to start up a new business, which of the following should you do?

    A. Make all payments on time and in full until the loan is repaid.

    B. Use the money for frivolous wants that fulfill your personal interests.

    C. Avoid putting the terms of the loan in writing to keep things flexible between you and your friend.

    D. Skip payments on the loan.

10. Which of the following does not represent responsible credit card use for a business owner?

    A. Paying only a portion of the balance by the due date each month.

    B. Using the credit card to make all your business's purchases.

    C. Applying for several credit cards to increase your overall credit limit.

    D. All of the above.

Name:_____ Date:_____ Period: _____

Apply It

Make out each of the following checks according to the information provided:

1. You purchased office supplies from Office Depot for $118.97.

2. You paid Green Graphic Design $245.00 to create and design a logo for your business.

166   Chapter 21

Name:_____ Date:_____ Period: _____

Write Now

Imagine you are writing an advice column for entrepreneurs. Write a response to each of the following letters.

Dear Entrepreneurship Expert,

I want to open up a store that sells comic books and comic-related gifts and souvenirs. I have a huge collection of items and have found a comic book supplier who is willing to work with me. I am planning on visiting the local bank and applying for a loan to help me get my business up and running. But, I have been told that I need to establish credit first. What does this mean and how do I go about it?

Sincerely,

Comic Looking for Relief

Dear Comic Looking for Relief,

Entrepreneurship Workbook

Dear Entrepreneurship Expert,

I have been running my own auto detailing business for the last eight months. I received a loan from the Small Business Administration to help pay for the business's start-up costs but I'm having trouble keeping up with my payments on the loan. It seems like there is never enough money to make my payments and cover my other expenses as well. How can I better manage my debt?

Sincerely,

Distressed over Debt

Dear Distressed over Debt,

Name:_____ Date:_____ Period: _____

Short Answer

Managing credit is an important skill to have if you are running a business. Answer the following questions about credit.

1. How can you establish credit?

   _____
   _____
   _____

2. Why is it important to establish credit?

   _____
   _____
   _____

3. What is a credit report? Why is it important?

   _____
   _____
   _____

4. How can you find out what your credit report says?

   _____
   _____
   _____

5. How can you protect your credit?

   _____
   _____
   _____

6. What are some guidelines for managing credit?

   _____
   _____
   _____

Name:_____ Date:_____ Period:_____

Fill in the Blank

Complete each statement with a term from the box.

Asset	IRS	Returns
Consumption	Loan	State
Federal	Local	Tax
FTC	Progressive	Tax deductions
Income	Regressive	Taxable income

1. _____ taxes are based on wages and other earnings.
2. _____ taxes are based on things we already own, such as houses or cars.
3. _____ taxes are based on things we buy, such as computers or gasoline.
4. Income, Social Security, and fuel taxes are examples of taxes paid to the _____ government.
5. Each _____ sets its own sales tax rate.
6. Property taxes are an example of taxes paid to the _____ government.
7. The United States has a(n) _____ tax system, which means the more you earn, the more you pay.
8. _____ are expenses taken out of your income on which you do not have to pay taxes.
9. Income tax _____ are forms on which you calculate the amount of income tax you owe.
10. The _____ is the federal agency responsible for collecting federal taxes.
11. A(n) _____ is money paid to the government in exchange for the public resources it provides.
12. To calculate your _____, you add up all of your income and then subtract tax deductions.

170   Chapter 21

Name:_____ Date:_____ Period: _____

Critical Thinking

It is important to keep your personal and business information safe. Read the following questions and record your answers below.

1. What have you heard or what do you know about identity theft?

   _____
   _____
   _____

2. Why do you think it has become more common today?

   _____
   _____
   _____

3. What can you do to protect yourself when it comes to your personal records?

   _____
   _____
   _____

4. What should you do if you lose your wallet or it is stolen?

   _____
   _____
   _____

5. What can you do to protect yourself online?

   _____
   _____
   _____

6. Social networking sites have become a common means of communication today. Do you think they pose risks for identity theft? Explain.

   _____
   _____
   _____

Chapter 22: Basic Economics

Name: _____ Date: _____ Period: _____

Crossword

Across:
1. Measures changes in the prices of goods and services
2. Study of how people produce, distribute, and use goods and services
7. Resources that cannot be replaced
9. Limit on the quantity of a product that can be imported into a country
10. Workers who make goods and provide services
11. Goods that are used in production, such as factories, tools and computers
13. When the average price of goods goes up sharply
14. When supply available does not meet demand
19. Amount of goods and services a business is willing to sell at a specified price and time
20. Downturn in the economy
21. Hiring people in other countries to do certain jobs
22. All natural resources including forests, minerals, and water
23. Fee similar to a tax that importers pay on goods they import
24. When there is never enough of everything to satisfy everyone completely

Down:
1. People who purchase and use goods and services
3. Resources that can be used again and again
4. When a business has no competition and controls all the supply and demand for the product or service it sells
5. Economy in which suppliers produce whatever goods and services they want to and set prices based on what consumers are willing to pay
6. Growing integration of the world's economies
8. When supply is greater than demand
11. Economy in which the government owns or manages the nation's resources and businesses
12. Amount of money that exceeds the cost of a business's expenses
13. Goods and services that are brought into the country from foreign suppliers
15. Total value of all goods and services produced in a country
16. Measure of how your resources create happiness or satisfaction
17. Goods or services sent from one country and sold in another
18. Quantity of goods and services consumers are willing to buy at a specific time and a specific price

Possible Answers:

CPI	GDP	monopoly	scarcity
capital	globalization	nonrenewable	shortage
command	imports	offshoring	supply
consumers	inflation	profit	surplus
demand	labor	quota	tariff
economics	land	recession	utility
exports	market	renewable	

Entrepreneurship Workbook

Name:_____ Date:_____ Period: _____

True or False

Circle whether each statement is true or false.
1. True   False   Resources that make you happy or bring you satisfaction have low utility.
2. True   False   Sustainable economic development does not harm society or the environment.
3. True   False   Businesses that make or provide goods and services are considered consumers.
4. True   False   When the unemployment rate is high, more people are working, which means they are spending more.
5. True   False   Typically, prices of products and services go down when the supply is greater than the demand.

Short Answer

Answer the questions below about supply and demand.
1. What is "supply?"
   _____
   _____

2. What is "demand?"
   _____
   _____

3. What is the law of supply and demand?
   _____
   _____

4. Would a business want to sell more or less of its products at a higher price? Explain.
   _____
   _____
   _____

5. Would consumers want to buy more or less of a product at a lower price? Explain.
   _____
   _____
   _____

Name:_____ Date:_____ Period: _____

Critical Thinking

1. Is there a product that you would stop buying when its price goes up, even a little? Explain.
   _____
   _____
   _____

2. Is there a product that you would keep buying even if its price rose considerably? Explain.
   _____
   _____
   _____

3. What is likely to happen to the price of air conditioners in colder months of the year?
   _____
   _____
   _____

4. What would you expect to happen to the demand for gasoline if everyone began using electric cars?
   _____
   _____
   _____

5. How would you expect the use of electric cars to affect the availability of gasoline and its price?
   _____
   _____
   _____

6. Explain why you would or would not invest in an ice cream company that sold its products only in Alaska.
   _____
   _____
   _____

7. You own a dairy and soybean farm in Wisconsin. You spend half the time farming soybeans and the other half taking care of the cows. The price of milk has just gone up 50 cents a gallon. What signal is the market sending?

8. You own a roller rink with a "1960s" theme that plays rock-and-roll music from that decade. Your rink has been very successful for the last few years, but lately, it has not drawn as many customers. People are going instead to the new rink across town that plays hip hop and rap music for patrons to skate to. You've tried lowering your admission price, but you are still losing money every day. What signal is the market sending you? What are some ways you could respond?

Name:_____ Date:_____ Period: _____

Critical Thinking

Sustainability has become a hot topic at home, at school, and in the workplace. Answer the questions below about sustainability.

1. What could you and your family do to reduce the energy costs in your home?

   _____
   _____
   _____
   _____
   _____

2. What could you and your classmates do to reduce the amount of trash and garbage you generate?

   _____
   _____
   _____
   _____
   _____

3. What could you and your co-workers do to reduce pollution?

   _____
   _____
   _____
   _____
   _____

4. What does "going green" mean to you?

   _____
   _____
   _____
   _____
   _____

Name:_____ Date:_____ Period: _____

Teamwork

Working in small groups, discuss the following questions about competition and record your answers below. Be prepared to discuss your answers in class.

1. What types of competition do you face in school?
   _____
   _____
   _____
   _____

2. How does competition at school help you develop and improve your skills and abilities?
   _____
   _____
   _____
   _____

3. How do you benefit from competition among companies to get your business?
   _____
   _____
   _____
   _____

4. How would the absence of competition for a product or service affect its price?
   _____
   _____
   _____
   _____

5. How would the absence of competition for a product or service affect its quality?
   _____
   _____
   _____
   _____

Name:_____ Date:_____ Period: _____

Analysis

List three businesses from which you buy products or services. (These can include stores, restaurants, online businesses, companies that provide services, such as a hair salon or a lawn care company, etc.) Then, list two competitors of the business and explain why you do *not* buy the same products or services from them.

Business #1:

    Competitor: _____

    _____

    Competitor: _____

    _____

Business #2:

    Competitor: _____

    _____

    Competitor: _____

    _____

Business #3:

    Competitor: _____

    _____

    Competitor: _____

    _____

What type of business would you like to start?

_____

_____

_____

List all the businesses you can think of that would be your competitors.

_____

_____

_____

Chapter 23: Basic Business Financial Management

Name:_____ Date:_____ Period: _____

True or False

Circle whether each statement is true or false.

1. True   False   Income statements can only be prepared one time a year.
2. True   False   If a business's sales are less than its expenses, the income statement will show a profit.
3. True   False   If a company has revenues of $40,500 and expenses of $22,000, than it is "in the black."
4. True   False   The balance sheet for a financially healthy business should show that its assets are higher than its liabilities and owner's equity.
5. True   False   Salaries and wages a business pays are considered cash outflows.
6. True   False   A financially healthy company should be generating most of its revenue through loans it obtains from different lenders.
7. True   False   The IRS requires that all businesses keep records for its tax collecting purposes.
8. True   False   If a company is publicly traded, its financial records must be made public.
9. True   False   It is legal for an accountant to change his employer's sales numbers in order to make the business look better.

Matching

Indicate on which financial statement you would find each item by writing the letter on the blank.

____ 1. Assets   B. Balance Sheet
____ 2. Expenses   C. Cash Flow Statement
____ 3. Net Profit/Loss   I. Income Statement
____ 4. Liabilities
____ 5. Cash Receipts
____ 6. Revenue
____ 7. Owner's Equity
____ 8. Dividends Received/Paid

Name:_____ Date:_____ Period: _____

Short Answer

Write your answer to each question in the space provided.

1. What is accounting?

   _____
   _____
   _____
   _____

2. How is accounting used by businesses?

   _____
   _____
   _____
   _____

3. Why should an entrepreneur know basic accounting principles?

   _____
   _____
   _____
   _____

4. What could a "would-be" entrepreneur do while in school to learn more about basic accounting principles?

   _____
   _____
   _____
   _____

Name:_____ Date:_____ Period: _____

Apply It

You have a business selling caps. For the month of June, you bought 20 caps for $5 each and sold them all at $10 each. You paid $40 in commissions to your brother to help you sell them, and you spent $20 on posters as advertising. Your taxes are 20% of your pre-tax profit. Prepare your income statement, and then answer the questions that follow.

Income Statement

Month _____

REVENUE

    Gross Sales $ _____

    Sales Returns   _____

    Net Sales   _____

COST OF GOODS MANUFACURED AND SOLD

    Materials $ _____

    Labor   _____

    Total Cost of Goods Sold   _____

GROSS PROFIT $ _____

OPERATING EXPENSES

    Advertising $ _____

    Commissions   _____

    Depreciation   _____

    Insurance   _____

    Rent   _____

    Utilities   _____

    Salaries   _____

    Total Expenses   _____

PRE-TAX PROFIT $ _____

    Taxes (20%)   _____

NET PROFIT/LOSS $ _____

1. What is the cost of goods sold? Explain.

2. Did you have a net profit or net loss for the month of June? How did you calculate this number?

3. What is the difference between gross profit and net profit?

4. How much did you pay in taxes? How did you calculate this number?

5. What might you do to increase your net profits in the future?

Name:_____ Date:_____ Period:_____

Short Answer

Write your answer to each question in the space provided.

1. What is the purpose of a balance sheet?

   _____
   _____
   _____
   _____

2. What are assets?

   _____
   _____
   _____
   _____

3. What are liabilities?

   _____
   _____
   _____
   _____

4. What is owner's equity?

   _____
   _____
   _____
   _____

Name:_____ Date:_____ Period: _____

Apply It

Prepare a balance sheet using the information given for each of the scenarios below.

You started a small business making and selling silk-screened T-shirts. You used $200 in savings to buy a silk-screening machine to make the shirts (capital equipment). You borrowed $100 from your parents (short-term liability) to buy 10 shirts wholesale at $2.50 each (inventory). You deposited the remaining money in your business's checking account (cash). Prepare your balance sheet.

Balance Sheet

ASSETS		LIABILITIES	
Cash:	$ _____	Short-Term Liabilities:	$ _____
Inventory:	_____	Long-Term Liabilities:	_____
Capital Equipment:	_____	**TOTAL LIABILITIES**	$ _____
Other Assets	_____	**OWNER'S EQUITY (OE)**	$ _____
TOTAL ASSETS	$ _____	**TOTAL LIABILITIES + OE**	$ _____

You started a jewelry business by saving $200 from your job (owner's equity) and borrowing $300 to be paid back in six months (short-term liability). You spent $300 on jewelry (inventory) and $75 on jewelry making tools (capital equipment). You deposited the remaining $125 from your original investment in your business's checking account (cash). You have not made any sales yet. Prepare your balance sheet.

Balance Sheet

ASSETS		LIABILITIES	
Cash:	$ _____	Short-Term Liabilities:	$ _____
Inventory:	_____	Long-Term Liabilities:	_____
Capital Equipment:	_____	**TOTAL LIABILITIES**	$ _____
Other Assets	_____	**OWNER'S EQUITY (OE)**	$ _____
TOTAL ASSETS	$ _____	**TOTAL LIABILITIES + OE**	$ _____

Name:_____ Date:_____ Period: _____

Critical Thinking

Review the Cash Flow Statement below, and then answer the questions that follow it.

Cash Flow Statement		
Beginning Cash Balance:		$7,325.00
Cash Inflow		
Investment:	$1,055.00	
Sales:	$9,050.00	
Total Cash Inflow:	$10,105.00	$_____
Cash Outflow		
Inventory:	$3,600.00	
Variable Costs:	$1,480.00	
Fixed Costs:	$2,900.00	
Equipment:	$1,100.00	
Other Outflows:	$875.00	
Total Cash Outflow:	$_____	$_____
Net Cash Flow:		$_____
Ending Cash Balance:		$_____

1. What is the total cash inflow? How did you calculate this number?

   _____

   _____

2. What is the total cash outflow? How did you calculate this number?

   _____

   _____

3. What is the Ending Cash Balance? How did you calculate this number? Did the business have a positive or negative cash flow?

   _____

   _____

Chapter 24: Financial Calculations for Business

Name:_____ Date:_____ Period: _____

Economics of One Unit

Answer each of the following questions in the space provided.

1. What is the economics of one unit?

   _____
   _____

2. Why should entrepreneurs study the economics of one unit of sale for their businesses?

   _____
   _____

3. List at least three expenses that might be included in a business's cost of goods sold.

   _____
   _____
   _____

4. What is the unit of sale in a restaurant that serves lunch and dinner meals?

   _____

5. What is the unit of sale in a store that sells new CDs?

   _____

6. What is the unit of sale for a barber?

   _____

7. What is the unit of sale for a daycare center that charges according to the number of hours a child is under their care?

   _____

Entrepreneurship Workbook

8. What is the average sale per customer for a restaurant that serves 200 customers a day and takes in sales revenue of $3,000?

   _____

   _____

9. Pete, the owner of The Funky DJ, provides DJ services to parties and other social events in his community. He charges $40 per hour. He rents a double turntable from his older brother at $10 per hour every time he works.

   What is the unit of sale? _____

   What is the gross profit per unit? _____

   _____

10. Sue, of Sue's Sandwich Stop, sells sandwich and soda combos from a sidewalk cart in a popular park near her house. She sets up her cart in the summers to raise money for college. Last month, she sold $1,000 worth of product to 100 customers. Her cost of goods sold is $4 per sandwich and $1 per soda.

    What is the unit of sale? _____

    What is the gross profit per unit? _____

    _____

11. Della gives riding lessons at her grandparents' horse farm. In a typical five-day work week, she gives 15 lessons and makes $300. Her cost of goods sold is $3.50 per lesson.

    What is the unit of sale? _____

    What is the gross profit per unit? _____

    _____

12. You buy posters of celebrities from a wholesaler at $3 per poster, poster frames for $7 each from a different wholesaler, and sell the framed poster for $20.

    What is the unit of sale? _____

    What is the gross profit per unit? _____

    _____

Name:_____ Date:_____ Period: _____

Break-Even Analysis

1. Describe how finding your business's break-even point would help you operate your business.

   _____
   _____
   _____

2. Define *gross profit per unit*.

   _____
   _____
   _____

3. Calculate the gross profit per unit of the following items.

Item	Selling Price per Unit	Cost of Goods Sold per Unit	Gross Profit per Unit (show your work here)
T-shirt	$16.00	$11.50	
Box of Gift Cards	$8.00	$5.95	
Manicure	$24.00	$9.75	
3-Pound Bag of Dog Biscuits	$6.00	$4.89	
1 Hour of Accounting Services	$45.00	$16.00	

Entrepreneurship Workbook **189**

4. Using the data you calculated in #3 on the previous page, apply the break-even formula to find the break-even unit for each item.

Item	Operating Expenses	Gross Profit per Unit (fill in from #3 table)	Break-Even Unit (show your work here; round up to the nearest whole number)
T-shirt	$95.00		
Box of Gift Cards	$128.00		
Manicure	$44.00		
3-Pound Bag of Dog Biscuits	$12.00		
1 Hour of Accounting Services	$225.00		

Forecasting Cash Flow

Complete the cash budget below.

Cash Budget for the Month of July			
Cash Inflows	Forecast	Actual	Difference (show your work here)
Cash sales	$1,000.00	$724.89	
Credit collections	$1,200.00	$758.99	
Bank loans	$5,000.00	$5,000.00	
Other income	$500.00	$450.00	
Total Cash Inflows	$ _____	$ _____	$ _____

Cash Outflows	Forecast	Actual	Difference
Estimated variable expenses	$450.00	$300.00	
Insurance	$445.00	$438.00	
Salaries	$4,000.00	$4,000.00	
Advertising	$250.00	$199.00	
Interest	$300.00	$279.00	
Utilities	$250.00	$197.00	
Rent	$1,500.00	$1,500.00	
Other Fixed Expenses	$250.00	$235.00	
Total Cash Outflows	$ _____	$ _____	$ _____

CASH AVAILABLE	$ _____	$ _____	$ _____

1. Is the cash flow for the month of July positive or negative? By what amount is it positive or negative?

   _____
   _____

2. List ways a business can increase cash inflows.

   _____
   _____
   _____

3. List ways a business can decrease cash outflows.

   _____
   _____
   _____

Name:_____ Date:_____ Period: _____

Analysis

Review the income statement shown below, and then answer the questions that follow.

Income Statement
Month: June

REVENUE
    Gross Sales $200.00
    Sales Returns   0
    Net Sales $200.00

COST OF GOODS MANUFACURED AND SOLD
    Materials $100.00
    Labor   0
    Total Cost of Goods Sold   100.00

GROSS PROFIT $100.00

OPERATING EXPENSES
    Advertising $ 20.00
    Commissions   40.00
    Depreciation   0
    Insurance   0
    Rent   0
    Utilities   0
    Salaries   0
    Total Expenses   60.00

PRE-TAX PROFIT $ 40.00
    Taxes (20%)   8.00

NET PROFIT/LOSS $ 32.00

1. Calculate the operating ratio. Show your work in the space below.

2. Calculate the return on sales. Show your work in the space below.

Review the balance sheet shown below, and then answer the questions that follow.

Balance Sheet

ASSETS		LIABILITIES	
Cash:	$125.00	Short-Term Liabilities:	$300.00
Inventory:	300.00	Long-Term Liabilities:	0
Capital Equipment:	75.00	**TOTAL LIABILITIES**	$300.00
Other Assets	0	**OWNER'S EQUITY (OE)**	$200.00
TOTAL ASSETS	$500.00	**TOTAL LIABILITIES + OE**	$500.00

1. Calculate the debt ratio. Show your work in the space below.

2. Calculate the debt-to-equity ratio. Show your work in the space below.

3. What is *return on investment*?

4. If this business's first quarterly income statement showed a net profit of $285 and the initial investment equaled the owner's equity, what is its return on investment? Show your work in the space below. Would you consider this a good ROI?

Entrepreneurship Workbook